B R E N D A

Not My Will

Finding Peace with Things You Can't Change

To
Rose,
Grace and
peace be with you.
Brenda
Poinsett

Other books by Brenda Poinsett

Wonder Women of the Bible:
Heroes of Yesterday Who Inspire Us Today

Holiday Living: Using Year-Round Holidays
to Build Faith and Family

BRENDA POINSETT

Not My Will

Finding Peace with Things You Can't Change

NEW HOPE
PUBLISHERS
Gospel-Centered. Missions-Driven.

BIRMINGHAM, ALABAMA

New Hope® Publishers
P. O. Box 12065
Birmingham, AL 35202-2065
NewHopeDigital.com
New Hope Publishers is a division of WMU®.

Library of Congress Control Number: 2013936961

Unless otherwise indicated, all Scripture quotations in this publication are from the Good News Translation—Second Edition Copyright © 1992 by American Bible Society. Used by permission.

Scripture quotations marked KJV are taken from The Holy Bible, King James Version.

Scripture quotations marked NASB are taken from the New American Standard Bible®, Copyright © 1960, 1962, 1963, 1968, 1971, 1972, 1973, 1975, 1977, 1995 by The Lockman Foundation. Used by permission.

Scripture quotations marked NIV are taken from the HOLY BIBLE, NEW INTERNATIONAL VERSION®. NIV®. Copyright©1973, 1978, 1984 by International Bible Society. Used by permission of Zondervan. All rights reserved.

Scripture quotations marked NLT are taken from the Holy Bible, New Living Translation, copyright © 1996. Used by permission of Tyndale House Publishers, Inc., Wheaton, Illinois. All rights reserved.

Scripture quotations marked Phillips are taken from THE NEW TESTAMENT IN MODERN ENGLISH, Revised Edition, J. B. Phillips, translator. © J. B. Phillips 1958, 1960, 1972. By permission of Macmillan Publishing Co., Inc.

Scripture quotations marked Williams are taken from the Williams New Testament, The New Testament in the Language of the People, by Charles B. Williams. Copyright © 1937, 1966, 1986 by Holman Bible Publishers. Used by permission.

Scripture quotations marked TLB are taken from *The Living Bible*, copyright© 1971. Used by permission of Tyndale House Publishers, Inc., Wheaton, IL. All rights reserved.

Scripture quotations marked NCV are taken from the New Century Version®. Copyright © 1987, 1988, 1991 by Word Publishing, a division of Thomas Nelson, Inc. Used by permission. All rights reserved.

ISBN-10: 1-59669-387-8
ISBN-13: 978-1-59669-387-6

N134128 • 0913 • 3M1

Dedicated to

BAP and JLS

Table of Contents

Note to the Reader

When Ruth and her mother-in-law, Naomi, were destitute, she went to gather grain to help them get by. "Her hap was to light on a part of the field belonging unto Boaz" (Ruth 2:3 KJV). Boaz just happened to be in a position to rescue these two women, and he did. Her chance encounter with Boaz started a chain of events that would transform her and Naomi's life.

Happenstance like this played a part in my discovering a book that would broaden my horizons and eventually help me deal with things I couldn't change. That life would include some things like this hadn't occurred to me yet. At the time, I was in the library trying to get a rough draft written for my first book, *Prayerfully Yours*. Needing to stretch, I wandered around and ended up in the stacks looking at the titles of books on prayer. I came across one called *Messages on Prayer*, not a showy title, and I might have passed by it, except the author's name caught my eye. It was written by B. H. Carroll, the founder and first president of the seminary I attended.

I pulled out the book and scanned the table of contents. Two of the messages were about Jesus' prayer life. *Hmm*, I thought, *Jesus had a prayer life?* Of course, I knew He prayed, but a real prayer life? Weren't His prayers just examples for us to follow? He didn't really need to pray, did He? Didn't He have all the resources of heaven at His disposal? Couldn't God have simply supplied the power and direction Jesus needed without His having to ask?

After finishing *Prayerfully Yours*, I checked out *Messages on Prayer* and began studying Jesus' prayer life. Following Carroll's outline, I worked through each prayer, supplementing and amplifying each one with other resources. I found the subject so interesting that I wanted to pull the material together, organize it and write about it. Two editors later I signed a contract for the manuscript that became *When Jesus Prayed*.

As I pulled together my research and began writing, something dawned on me. About five chapters in, I realized there was something Jesus' prayers couldn't change. On page 49, I wrote, "Jesus was on his way to the Cross. His destiny was to be the suffering Messiah. No amount of praying would change that. His dying on the Cross was a voluntary act; but, in another sense, it wasn't. If he wanted to be the obedient Son, there was only one way before him. His destiny was an unchangeable certainty."

Perhaps I noticed this unchangeable because I was beginning to see things in my own life that couldn't be changed—unchangeable problems! While I didn't go ahead and write about these problems in *When Jesus Prayed*, what I learned became readily applicable and helpful. As I identified with Him, Jesus became my template for getting through those problems. When I followed His example, I could accept what I couldn't change and could move forward in life with peace and joy. This was good news, and I wanted to share it so I wrote *Not My Will but Thine: Coming to Terms with Things You Can't Change*. This is a revision of that book; the lessons are still needed.

Consequently, much of what you read in this book will be directly taken from *Not My Will but Thine*. Some additional informative paragraphs are from *Reaching Heaven: Discovering the Cornerstones of Jesus' Prayer*, another book I've written. In *Reaching Heaven*, Jesus' prayers aren't in chronological order like they were in *When Jesus Prayed* and *Not My Will but Thine*. Rather the book groups His prayers under four categories: withdrawal, thanksgiving, honesty, and intercession, and they are given a broader application rather than being specifically applied to unchangeables.

I've also stayed with the storyline of my own circumstances—the ones where I first applied the principles I learned while writing *When Jesus Prayed*. In addition to using my life for illustrating the lessons I learned from Jesus, I also use the examples and words of others who dealt with things that couldn't be changed. I'm grateful to friends such as Russ, Peggy, Allan, and others for letting me share bits and pieces from their struggles with unchangeables. For the most part, the names of friends have been changed, and sometimes a few details altered to protect their privacy. I've also used quotes and insights from people who have shared their stories in magazines and books. I'm thankful for their insights, and I'm thankful New Hope® wanted to publish this revision. I'm grateful for the help of Andrea Mullins, Joyce Dinkins, Melissa Hall, Tina Atchenson, and many others at New Hope for making *Not My Will* possible.

I'm sure there are many ways of coming to terms with things you can't change. Ministers, psychologists, psychiatrists, counselors, and other writers all have wisdom to offer. What I'm sharing is from the perspective of a believer who latched onto Jesus and walked with Him from His baptism to the Cross. This helped me and continues to help me. I doubt that I would have ever figured this out if I hadn't run across B. H. Carroll's book.

Yes, happenstance led me to start studying Jesus' prayer life, but it is a deliberate choice that prompts me to apply what I learned. I'm a woman who craves peace, who wants to feel fully alive, and who wants to be hopeful rather than pessimistic. These things are possible when I pray like Jesus prayed.

How about you? Are you struggling with something you can't change? Do you want peace and joy? Do you want to embrace the future? If so, I invite you to read this book, get to know Jesus better, and make peace with what you can't change.

Part I

The Dilemma
Struggling with What We Can't Change

*"Father, if thou be willing,
remove this cup from me;
nevertheless not my will,
but thine, be done."*

Luke 22:42 (KJV)

Chapter 1

In the Jaws of a Vise

"It is not part of the Christian hope to look for a life in which a man is saved from all trouble and distress; the Christian hope is that a man in Christ can endure any kind of trouble and distress, and remain erect all through them, and come out to glory on the other side."[1]

William Barclay

When Russ gave 16-year-old Sara permission to cruise around town with her friends, he didn't dream that three hours later, she would look as though she had been placed in a meat grinder and broken to pieces.

On an unfamiliar road, the driver of the car Sara was in ran a stop sign and hit two trees. Sara suffered massive deep cuts all over her body. Her teeth and gums were visible through the gaping cuts to her jaws, neck, and face. Her left lung had collapsed, her pelvis was broken. She had deep lacerations to her arms and legs with issue protruding from the cuts. Russ just stood looking at his daughter in disbelief as he realized there was nothing he could do.

PEGGY'S FINGERS WERE OFTEN INFECTED, and the infection didn't readily respond to treatment. To find out why the infection kept recurring, Peggy underwent many medical tests. The resulting diagnosis: scleroderma.

Peggy had never heard of scleroderma before. When her doctor explained it to her, he said, "Scleroderma is not a fatal disease. You will be able to handle all the symptoms as they come up. What you will mostly be aware of is not getting any wrinkles as you age."

Peggy thought, *Gee, I can handle this!*

The doctor suggested she write the Scleroderma Foundation for more information. From the information she received, Peggy discovered she was facing an ugly, disabling, and eventually fatal disease. There was no known cure.

MARK HAD A PASSION FOR BOOKS; his enthusiasm made him a successful area sales representative for a major book publisher. The publisher, though, took a number of risky ventures; the company lost money. To recover, sales were turned over to an outside agency, and all the sales representatives were fired. Mark cleaned out his desk, drove home, and went to bed. Feigning sickness, he stayed there for three days before he told his wife he had been fired.

CAITLIN, A COLLEGE STUDENT, noticed that many of those in her Christian student group had trouble conversing with and being comfortable around non-Christians. Caitlin didn't; she moved easily among Christians and non-Christians. She never actually compromised her beliefs, but she was often coy in what she revealed and didn't reveal. She saw herself as savvy and sophisticated because she successfully moved in and out of both groups.

At the Christian student group's fall retreat, Caitlin was unexpectedly challenged by the emphasis on holy living. Her heart stirred the way it had some nine years earlier when she became a Christian. Realizing that God was speaking to her, she thought, *Oh God, please don't ask me to change.* I can't handle being different.

GREG HAD A GOAL that he carried within himself; he knew that some day he was going to be a professional baseball player. This goal was nurtured by his friends and coaches who told him how good he was and by his father who often said, "Son, you can be anything you want to be."

After college, when he tried out for the pros, he was accepted by a farm club. Greg wasn't discouraged by this; he was a hard worker and saw this as a rung on the ladder to success. He was stunned when the manager called him in at the end of his first season and said, "Greg, I'm going to level with you. You don't have what it takes to make it in professional baseball. I advise you to start planning another career."

WHEN TOM, THE CHURCH'S YOUTH DIRECTOR, asked for adults under forty to chaperone the youth attending the state convention, 45-year-old Jill couldn't believe her ears. While she didn't work with the youth on a regular basis, she always volunteered to chaperone their out-of-town trips. She thought, *And now because of my age, I'm not capable any longer?* She couldn't stop thinking about it during the morning's sermon. She hated the thought of growing old and was going to fight it with all the resources she had.

After church, Tom saw Jill in the foyer. He asked, "Can I count on you to chaperone the youth convention? Startled, she just looked at him. Then she realized, He doesn't know how old I am. Oh, good! "Why sure, Tom, I'll be glad to help you out."

ALLAN AND RUTH were having one of those end-of-the-day, leisurely kind of conversations that only people who have been married a long time can have. They talked about things that mattered and also inconsequential things, often blending one with the other. Sometimes there were comfortable pauses of silence, as each dealt with his or her own thoughts. Then one of them would pick up the conversation again. It was their way of unwinding before they fell asleep. During an unusually long period of silence, Allan heard some strange gurgling sounds from Ruth's side of the bed. Allan said, "What is it, Ruth?" There was no answer. "Ruth, Ruth?" Allan turned on the light and saw a strange look on Ruth's face. He touched her and she didn't respond. He called 911. The emergency personnel came and rushed Ruth to the hospital where the attending physician pronounced her dead from an aneurysm.

AT FIRST GLANCE, these stories may seem unrelated, but they aren't. Sooner or later, we all come up against something we can't change.

Accidents. It may be something that comes as starkly and abruptly as Sara's accident, a natural disaster, or a violent act of crime. After the fact, these events cannot be changed.

Terminal illness. The future may seem like something that can't be changed for those like Peggy who have a terminal or incurable illness. Some people might want to argue with this label and say, "Miracles are always possible," but for many the miracles will not come.

Job termination. A person fired from his job may be able to change his future, but he can't change his past. He may want to push the Replay button on the recorder of life, but he will discover the Replay button doesn't work. Life cannot be replayed.

God's will. While we may be wrong in how we interpret God's will, the kind of life He wants us to live will not change. If we want to be God's obedient children, then we will do what He wants.

Personal limitations. The self-help books we devour, the seminars we attend, the magazines we read, and the educational and motivational videos we watch imply we can change our looks, our weight, our mood, our self-esteem, and our income. Like Greg's father told him, they tell us, "You can be anything you want to be!" But all of us can't; there's a limit to what we can change about ourselves.

Aging. That Jill was discouraged by Tom's age-specific request is understandable, nevertheless, she will have to come to grips some time with aging. Face-lifting, hair-dying, and weight-watching may camouflage the aging process. Exercise, nutrition, and hormone-replacement therapy may slow it down, but aging is inevitable.

Death. Many fitness fanatics may believe they can live forever, if only they eat right and get their 10K runs in every morning. The best nutrition and exercise program available may add two to seven years to life, but it will not change the fact of Hebrews 9:27, "And as it is appointed unto men once to die."

SOME PEOPLE MAY BE RELUCTANT to think in terms of what they can't change. They are optimists who see themselves in control of their destinies. They thrive on self-help material that continually assures them change is possible.

Christians especially may bristle at the idea of something being unchangeable. After all, we have the best self-help material available—the Bible. We are resurrection people; we are eternal optimists. One of our frequently quoted slogans is, "Prayer changes things."

Personally I'm addicted to self-help materials and to the power of prayer. I believe in the possibility of change; yet, as the examples of Russ, Peggy, Mark, Caitlin, Jill, Greg, and Allan illustrate, we come up against things we can't change.

When I started encountering things I couldn't change, I found a void in self-help literature; it centered on change. And I found my way of praying ineffective. I needed help in coping and in coming to terms with what I could not change.

Trapped in a vise

Coping with unchangeables involves struggle, more intense for some than for others. The struggle may involve feelings such as fragility, agitation, anxiety, insecurity, discouragement, fear, anger, despair, resentment, and grief. Left unresolved, these powerful emotions rob us of our peace of mind. Left unexpressed, they can cause us to become cynical about life or hopeless about the future.

Coping with what we can't change requires adjustment. Evaluation and restructuring may be in order. Choices will need to be made. Relationships may be affected, especially our relationship with God. We may feel like He abandoned us or betrayed us. We may decide God is untrustworthy, or we may feel like it is futile to continue to try to please Him.

Coming up against things we can't change is like being in the jaws of a vise.

As a child I liked to rummage around in my grand-father's messy workshop. One of the items that fascinated me was the vise. I picked up blocks of wood that were scattered on the floor and put them in the vise. I turned the crank until the block or blocks were tightly in place, sometimes squeezing extra hard. I tried various blocks, sometimes a combination of two. I was fascinated with how the vise held the blocks securely in place, and I was fascinated by the power I had over the blocks. I was in control.

When we come up against something we can't change, we aren't turning the crank. We're the block of wood in the vise! As its jaws move in on us, we struggle and push against them. The vise squeezes us into a position we don't want to be in. We can push and push, but these jaws won't budge. We want to escape, but we can't. How then do we live with what we can't change?

A solution

What we can't change is such a broad category that research doesn't show one solution that works for every person, which is just as well. If we had a research-based, fool-proof solution, we might become glib about people's struggles. Coping with what we can't change involves grappling with the harsh realities of life. To pin a snappy, three-point, works-every-time formula on that kind of struggle is to trivialize it. It minimizes a person's pain and ignores individual circumstances.

Coping strategies vary. Some are effective; others are ineffective. Some are healthy; others are unhealthy. Some people cope by denying there is a dilemma. Others count on time as the solution—over time, they assure themselves, they will forget about what they can't change. Some people withdraw. They don't want to have anything to do with others, and sometimes they don't want to have anything to do with God. Some try distracting themselves through activities; others try positive thinking. Some count on the counsel of friends, support groups, or psychotherapists. Others try to comfort themselves through legal prescription drugs or through illegal drugs or alcohol.

Some people seem to adjust readily to what they can't change, while others become weighed down by the struggle. Some become stuck—unwilling or unable to move forward into the future. They need someone whose hand they can hold and whose leadership they can trust to pull them out of the slough of despondency and help them regain the joy of living.

The person who helps can't be just anybody. It has to be someone who has struggled with something he couldn't change. Those of us trying to cope with what we can't change can relate best to someone who has also experienced the jaws of the vise and pushed against them.

The premise of this book is that Jesus is just such a person. It may be hard for some of us to believe that Jesus—God Incarnate—struggled with something He couldn't change. Jesus had the power of heaven at His disposal. He came to earth to initiate change and succeeded. He was an agent of change on many occasions; and yet there was one thing He couldn't change—Jesus couldn't change His destiny to die on the Cross.

Jesus was to be the suffering Messiah. His dying on the Cross was a voluntary act, but in another sense, it wasn't. If He wanted to be the obedient Son, there was only one way before Him—the way of the Cross.

From where we stand, Jesus' triumph was so certain that it looks like it was effortless and without strain. His courage was so calm, so sure, so seemingly inevitable, that it almost looks automatic. But if we move closer to Him, if we walk with Him from His baptism to the Cross, focusing on His prayer life, we will see that it wasn't automatic. He, too, struggled with what He could not change; therefore, we can relate to Him and trust His leadership.

Walking with Jesus

Jesus said, "He that followeth me shall not walk in darkness, but shall have the light of life" (John 8:12 KJV). When we walk with Jesus, He will light up our path. He will help us see more clearly what we are up against. He will help us see possibilities that we didn't even know existed. He will show us how we can cope with what we can't change.

If we want "the light of life," we must take the whole walk from Jesus' baptism to His death on the Cross. If we look at just one prayer Jesus prayed, we might not get the complete picture of what is involved in coping with what we can't change. We need the broad picture to understand the nature of our struggle.

Eventually, as we walk with Jesus, we will begin to identify with Him. A kinship will develop so we will be able to say along with Him, "Now is my soul troubled" (John 12:27 KJV). This kinship ignites hope—if Jesus struggled and endured, perhaps I can too.

Identification leads to imitation. We may see patterns in the way that He prayed—patterns that may provide the breakthrough we need to give us the peace we long for or restore the joy we lost. We may hear the words He used in prayer and make those words our words so they give voice to our agony and bring relief. We may note where He prayed and find new places to offer our own prayers. We may be surprised and yet relieved by His honesty; this may encourage us to express honestly our emotions to God. We may marvel at His gratitude during both good times and bad times and wonder if gratitude could play a part in resolving our own situation. When we pray as Jesus prayed, we will gain specific ways for coping with what we can't change.

Intimacy results when we walk with a person sharing his life experiences, when we hear his prayers, when we see things from his perspective, and when we hear his cries of anguish. In the "fellowship of his sufferings" we can know Jesus (Philippians 3:10 KJV) and find strength to live with what we cannot change.

From inspiration to application

How have I been trying to cope with what I can't change?

What will I gain by praying Jesus' way?

How are identification, imitation, and intimacy related?

*"O Light that followest all my way,
I yield my flick-'ring torch to thee."* [2]

Chapter 2

Finding the Right Label

"We can expect [God's] dealings with us to be unique. They will have a certain "ring" to them that is unlike any other experience we have ever had, yet somehow we will know, as Isaiah did, that this is God, the Holy One, revealing himself in his own way."[1]

John Claypool

As we begin our walk with Jesus, we need to ask, *When is something unchangeable and when is it not?* In a book that focuses on what we can't change, we wouldn't want to encourage anyone to call something unchangeable when it is. For good mental and spiritual health, none of us should be quick to label something unchangeable.

All of us need to see possibilities for change when they exist. Possibilities propel us forward, keeping us optimistic and hopeful. They enable us to believe we have some control over our lives. When we see ourselves as having no control, life is miserable.

The Bible teaches us to expect change. Jesus taught and encouraged us to believe all kinds of things are possible (Matthew 21:22; Mark 9:23; 11:22–24; Luke 17:6). To call something unchangeable too quickly is to close the door on faith-stretching experiences where miracles may occur. The possibility of change makes the Christian life exciting and dynamic so we need to ask, *What's changeable and what isn't?*

What's changeable

With some things, it is easy to apply the "changeable" label. We can readily recognize when earnest prayer would help us make changes.

- God, help me to manage my time so I can cover my workload and still have more time for my family.
- Father, I'm lonely. Help me to have the courage to make friends.
- Lord, help me find a way to break the tension between Jennifer and me. I don't want my relationship with her to be this way.

While the solutions may not be simple or come easily in each of these cases, the possibility for change is obvious. Time can be managed, friends can be made, and tension can be resolved.

What's not changeable

With some things, it's readily and painfully obvious we can't change them:

- After an automobile accident, we cannot go back and reduce our speed or take another route no matter how much we might fantasize about doing so.

- After a tornado destroys our home, we cannot go back to the way things were.
- After we lose a family member to death, we cannot bring that person back to life. The finality of death is hard to accept.

No matter what we do, or how much we try, we cannot change the fact that the accident occurred, the tornado came through our area, and that our loved one died. Reality says these things cannot be changed.

What's hard to label

In between what we can readily identify as changeable and what's obviously unchangeable are hard-to-label items. Divorce is an example. In many states it only takes one person wanting to get a divorce to get one. Does the nonconsenting spouse pray for God to restore the marriage, or does he or she ask God's help with adjusting to being single?

In *Hope Has Its Reasons*, Rebecca Manley Pippert tells the true story of a minister whose wife wanted out of the marriage. She said to her husband, "The marriage is not what I want, and I don't feel any love for you. I want out. I'm filing for a divorce."[2]

The minister had not seen it coming. Devastated and shocked, he said to his wife, "Please, don't do this. Let's try to make this work. Please don't get a divorce."[3]

The wife agreed not to file right away, but she did not stay with him. The minister began praying for his wife regularly and to love her in a way he hadn't before. Without his wife knowing, the minister often walked around her apartment at night and prayed for her, asking God to bless her. He saw his wife occasionally, but she held out no hope that they would reunite. Yet he believed that if he were constant and faithful, she would change her mind and return. Even though his faith in Jesus meant much to her, she still filed for divorce.

Following the divorce, the members of his church urged him to find a woman to share his life with, but he refused. Like the Old Testament prophet Hosea who followed God's instructions to love the wife who left him, this minister remained faithful and prayed daily for his wife.

Ten years after his wife left him, she came back, and they were reunited in marriage.

I marvel at this story, yet I'm reluctant to say to people who are unwillingly facing a divorce, "Hang in there. Keep praying and you will get your mate back." Even the minister acknowledged that this approach wouldn't necessarily be God's calling to everyone.

How does a person know whether to persevere in hoping a broken marriage will be mended or to accept it as over and move on with establishing a new life as a single person? How does someone like Peggy, diagnosed with scleroderma, know whether to accept the diagnosis and live with it or to believe in God for a miracle cure? Should Greg, who thought he was destined to be a professional baseball player, accept the advice of his manager to quit, or should he continue to try? How does a person know when to accept self-limitations and when to keep pursuing dreams?

In situations like these, knowing if something is changeable or unchangeable is difficult to evaluate. We want to hope for the best; we want to be optimistic. We don't want to surrender too soon if there is still some hope for change. We want to be faith-believing Christians who expect miracles. On the other hand, continually anticipating change might keep us from receiving the serenity and strength that comes with acceptance. It might keep us from making the necessary adjustments that would create new lives for ourselves.

Finding the label that applies is not easy. One day when our hopes are high, we call our situation changeable. A few days later, after some discouraging remarks from others or a stressful day, we may label it unchangeable. We may talk with friends, our pastor, or even a professional counselor, trying to find the definitive label.

What we seek is an inner assurance that we know without a doubt what the label is. The moment may come because we decide, *This is what I can live with, I have to make a decision. I can't go on like this.* It may come because it seems like the logical thing to do. Or, it may come for us in prayer as it did for Jesus after a long period of reflection, inner struggle, and deepening insight.

Jesus' situation

Exactly when Jesus' consciousness of His earthly role began, we don't know. Did He know it when He was a baby in the manger or as a small child? I can't imagine a three-year-old knowing He was the Son of God who would someday die on a cross for the salvation of men and women.

At some time in His youth, Jesus must have consciously discovered His unique relationship to God. Maybe it began with His first visit to the Temple in Jerusalem when He was 12 (Luke 2:41–50). Jesus was left behind by His parents when they started back to their home in Nazareth. When they discovered Jesus wasn't with them, Joseph and Mary went back to Jerusalem to look for Him. "After three days they found him in the temple courts, sitting among the teachers, listening to them and asking them questions . . . When his parents saw him, they were astonished. His mother said to him, 'Son, why have you treated us like this? Your father and I have been anxiously searching for you.'

"'Why were you searching for me?' he asked. 'Didn't you know I had to be in my Father's house?'" (Luke 2:46–49 NIV).

In his commentary on Luke, Ray Summers writes, "The question was literally, 'You were aware, were you not, that I must be in the things (or, in the places) of my Father?'" [4] The "places" would refer to the Temple buildings. Jesus' words indicate He had some understanding of His unique relationship with God; He was His Son. He belonged in God's house, yet He went back to Nazareth as a boy, obedient to His parents (Luke 2:51).

We don't know what happened in Jesus' life in the next 18 years other than He worked as a carpenter. While He worked, perhaps He pondered what His unique relationship with God the Father meant. What kind of work did God have for Him to do? Would God want Him to speak to people? How would He speak? Scathing like the prophets of old? Or gentle and understanding? How would people receive His message? Would He need to leave Nazareth? Would He face danger?

Some readers may be uncomfortable with the idea that Jesus would have asked these kinds of questions, and yet asking them is a normal part of maturing. If Jesus fully entered the human situation, then He had to grow into a consciousness of who He was, and He had to discover His mission. Luke said, "Jesus increased in wisdom and stature, and in favour with God and man" (Luke 2:52 KJV), and the writer of Hebrews said Jesus "learned through his sufferings to be obedient" (Hebrews 5:8) and "was made perfect" to become "the source of eternal salvation" (v. 9).

Jesus needed a moment when the questions would end, and He would know the direction of His future. What or who would be the catalyst for bringing His questions to an end?

The defining moment

That catalyst was John the Baptist. "John went throughout the whole territory of the Jordan River preaching, 'Turn away from your sins'" (Luke 3:3). Like the prophets of old, John boldly and dramatically confronted the people with their sins, and a revival occurred. When they repented, John baptized them. Jesus left Nazareth and joined those flocking to the Jordan (Matthew 3:13).

Jesus asked John to baptize him. As Jesus was being baptized, He prayed (Luke 3:21). Heaven opened, indicating that a revelation from God would follow. The Holy Spirit descended on Jesus "in bodily form like a dove" (v. 22 NIV), and a voice from heaven said, "Thou art my beloved Son; in thee I am well pleased" (Luke 3:22 KJV).

God's words were very significant. What He said was composed of two texts from the Old Testament. The texts were very familiar to Jews and would, therefore, have been familiar to Jesus.

"Thou art my Son" is from Psalm 2:7. This is a messianic psalm that foretold the triumph of the Messiah, God's anointed King. When Jesus heard these words, He knew Himself to be the King sent by God, the Messiah.

"In thee I am well pleased" refers to Isaiah's description of the servant of the Lord: "my servant, whom I uphold; mine elect, in whom my soul delighteth" (Isaiah 42:1 KJV). The portrait culminates in the sufferings of one who was wounded for our transgressions and bruised for our iniquities, the one on whom the chastisement of our peace fell, the one who was to be like a sheep dumb before its shearers (chap. 53).

So when Jesus heard the voice, He knew that He was God's chosen Messiah. He knew that the way for Him was the way of suffering and death. His future was defined.

Learning from Jesus

What can we learn from Jesus' experience that will help us define our situation?

Jesus put Himself in a place to hear from God. After His many hours of contemplation at Nazareth, Jesus needed to hear from God so He went to where God was visibly working. He went to where John the Baptist was having an impact and people were repenting of their sins. Jesus, who was without sin, didn't need to repent and be baptized. He was, though, ready to "fulfill all righteousness" (Matthew 3:15 KJV), to do what God wanted, so He put Himself in a place where God was working.

If we want a label for our dilemma—is it changeable or unchangeable?—we may need to move ourselves to a place where we can hear from God. The Bible says, "Draw nigh to God, and he will draw nigh to you" (James 4:8 KJV). The place in which we "draw nigh" can be an actual physical location or it can be a place of attitude.

After weeks of sleepless nights, stewing and brewing over his lost job, a friend persuaded Mark to go on a retreat. At first his emotions and spirit felt sealed off. He thought, *This is a waste of time. I should be home working on job applications so I can return to book selling.* Mark liked to sing, so he joined in with the others at the retreat. Then the leader called on him to pray. Little by little through various retreat activities, Mark unzipped his heart. Thirty-six hours later, when he was praying under a tree by the lake, Mark heard God speak, "Mark, I want you to embark on a new adventure. I have a new career in mind for you." Mark left the retreat relieved. On Monday he enrolled in the local community college to prepare for a new career.

Instead of moving ourselves to a physical place like a retreat site, we may have to move ourselves to a place of new attitude. We may have to move ourselves to a willingness to hear what God has to say. The first place—a physical place—is easier to reach than the second. It may take us a while to get to the attitude place. Before we arrive, we may have to ask ourselves, *Do I really want to put a label on what I am struggling with? Do I really want to conclude if it is changeable or unchangeable? Or would I rather keep on being indecisive about it, continuing back and forth in my mind?*

Jesus prayed. Moving to a place to hear from God means we're going to commune with Him. At John's revival scene, as he was being baptized, Jesus prayed. Why did Jesus need to pray? Couldn't God have simply supplied the power and direction Jesus needed without His having to ask? To answer this question, we need to remember why we all need to ask. Our asking opens our wills to God, giving Him the channel He needs to respond. Asking indicates a willingness to receive.

Jesus was made like us; therefore, He needed to open His will to God just as any of us do in order to let God respond to us and work through us. To suppose that Jesus' divinity freed Him from operating under the limitations that we do is to undermine the truth of John 1:14: "The Word became a human being and, full of grace and truth, lived among us."

Luke's description of Jesus' praying at His baptism sounds short and sweet; therefore, we might be tempted to think as we follow Jesus' example that a short, verbal prayer will gain us a label. For some, it may be so simple. For others, though, it may take some time and effort. We may have to repeatedly put ourselves in a place to hear from God before the label becomes clear. Many of my labeling experiences have been this way, which is reflected in my prayer journal. But the journal also shows that the answer does eventually come. A day arrives when I know what I'm dealing with is changeable or unchangeable. Perhaps the answer doesn't come as readily for me as it appeared to for Jesus because of the years of contemplation that preceded His prayer. He had been thinking about God's will for His life. He was ripe for an answer by the time He arrived in Judea to hear John preach, and when God spoke, Jesus heard His answer.

Jesus knew the Scriptures. Recognizing God's answer to our prayer for the right label is not as simple as recognizing God's answer to a request for something tangible. When we pray for three new members for our Bible study group, we know the prayer is answered when we have three new members. When we pray for money to repair our car, we know the prayer is answered when the money is in hand. When we pray for a label for our situation, the answer will be intangible. In our inner space, where we can't touch it, God's answer will come.

However, other voices also rumble around in our inner space, speaking to us. They want to answer us—cultural voices, the comments of family members and friends, and our own desires and wishes. How do we recognize God's voice from among the others?

At Jesus' baptism, He recognized God's answer because He knew the Scriptures and He knew their meaning. This is not to imply that God always answers with specific words and phrases from the Bible, but it does remind us that God always answers in line with His character as revealed in the Bible. God's answer to us will have a biblical precedent. We can, therefore, test any inner voice by asking, *Does this sound like something God would say?*

Not knowing what the Bible says should never keep us from praying, but if we are earnest about wanting God's label, we will study the Bible as well as pray. Prayer should not be an isolated area of our lives. It should be interwoven in the fabric of our lives right along with Bible study and other spiritual disciplines. Knowing what the Bible says will enhance our praying and improve our ability to recognize God's answers.

As we continue our walk with Jesus, we'll see these three lessons from Jesus' first recorded prayer reinforced. We'll learn more about Jesus putting Himself in places to hear from God, about how He prayed, and about how He used the Scriptures.

In the meantime, practicing these three principles will enable us to define our situation. We'll receive God's label, something we don't want to miss. Our future direction will become clearer. We'll know whether to pursue change or whether to accept the unchangeable. Either way will not necessarily be easy, but we will have the inner certainty and confidence that comes when we know God has spoken to us. That's something I don't want to be without.

From inspiration to application

What dilemma am I currently facing?

How am I labeling it? How are others labeling it?

_____ Changeable?
_____ Unchangeable?
_____ Uncertain?

Am I willing to move to a place to hear from God? Where might I go to discover God's label?

How will studying the Bible help me improve my ability to recognize God's voice?

*"God, grant me the serenity
To accept the things I cannot change,
Courage to change the things I can,
And the wisdom to know the difference."*

Chapter 3

Finding the Right Example

"If Christ had not felt the need to pray, He might seem to us, especially in the light of His sinlessness, an impressive and awesome figure, but He would not seem close to our common lives. We need to pray, and He means more to us because He, too, needed to pray."[1]

Elton Trueblood

L ois sat in Sue's living room and poured out her frustration. She said, "I can't concentrate any more. What am I going to do? I'm afraid I'm going to lose my job."

Tears began to flow as Lois described how she could no longer keep up with her co-workers. Occasionally she got up and paced the floor and then returned to the couch. Frightened and anxious, Lois said to Sue, "What's wrong with me?"

Sue took hold of both of Lois's hands, looked directly in her eyes and gently but firmly said, "Your husband died, you must accept it and move on."

That was exactly what Lois needed to do, but she bristled at Sue's suggestion. Sue made it sound so easy, as if there was nothing to it, no struggle involved.

Some of us have a similar view of what Jesus had to do. As one of my college students wrote in a paper, "Many people thought how much of a rebel Jesus was. The way I see it, he was simply doing the work of His Father, God. Jesus was labeled as a sinner because He healed many people on the Sabbath, but again, I believe He was just doing work for God. This was planned and meant to be according to God's word."

When God's voice spoke to Jesus at His baptism, Jesus learned what was before Him. He received His life's direction—a direction that involved suffering and the Cross. At the same time, the Holy Spirit descended on Jesus "in bodily form like a dove" (Luke 3:22 NIV) empowering Him. Herbert Lockyer, in *All the Prayers of the Bible*, said Jesus could not have commenced His ministry without the gift of the Holy Spirit. Doing God's will wasn't a simple matter for Jesus, and we need to realize this if we are going to identify with Him, learn from Him, and imitate Him.

The immediate struggle

After Jesus' baptism, the Spirit drove Jesus out into the wilderness (see Mark 1:12). It was time for some serious contemplation. He knew what the people's expectations were of a Messiah; He had heard many conversations about it in Nazareth. The people were looking for a liberator, someone who could win their freedom from Roman control and put them in charge. But was this what God wanted Him to do? What were His expectations? How would He usher in the kingdom John the Baptist was telling the people to expect? How was He to use the power He had been given?

In the wilderness, Jesus fasted (see Luke 4:2). To the Jews, fasting was a means by which strong emotions could be expressed. Fasting was connected with mourning and urgent supplication. At this time of heightened emotion and sensitivity, Jesus wrestled with the Tempter, and it was a tough fight.

Satan tried to get Jesus to doubt who He was. He said to Him "*If* you are God's Son, order these stones to turn to bread" (Matthew 4:3; author's italics) and "*If* you are God's Son, throw yourself" (v. 6) off the highest point of the temple.

Satan was trying to get Jesus to distrust Himself, to doubt His call, to question His task and His ability to complete it. It is as if he were saying, "How could a penniless, uneducated, Galilean carpenter like you possibly be the Messiah? Who ever heard of a Messiah suffering? Messiahs are supposed to be strong and victorious."

Jesus well knew the traditional and conventional ideas of what the Messiah would be like, and He knew God was calling Him to behave in a different, more revolutionary way. Would He do it? Not if Satan could help it.

Satin said to Jesus, "If you are God's Son, order these stones to turn to bread" (Matthew 4:3). I imagine that Jesus' hunger while He was fasting would make this a strong temptation, but there's more to it than satisfying hunger.

If He could turn stones into bread, then He could be a Bread Messiah. Bread was a precious commodity in Palestine. Only one-fifth of the land was arable under the best of conditions. This land was frequently plagued by extremes of drought and flood. In a place like this, bread was highly valued. One sure way for Jesus to persuade people to follow Him would be to give them bread.

To give men bread, though, would have meant bribing men to follow Him. If Jesus were to be God's Messiah, He could not persuade men to follow Him for what they could get out of Him. Jesus refuted Satan's temptation to turn stones into bread by quoting Scripture. Jesus answered, "It is written: 'Man does not live on bread alone, but on every word that comes from the mouth of God'" (Matthew 4:4 NIV).

Unsuccessful with the bread temptation, Satan tried again, and he made Scripture a part of his strategy! Satan took Jesus to the pinnacle of the temple. At the pinnacle, there was a sheer drop of 450 feet into the valley below. Satan said to Him, "If you are God's Son, throw yourself down, for the Scripture says, 'God will give orders to his angels about you; they will hold you up with their hands, so that not even your feet will be hurt on the stones'" (Matthew 4:6).

If He could leap down from that high pinnacle and land unharmed in the valley below, the people would be so startled, so impressed that they would follow Him. If He could do a thing like that, He would be the Spectacular Messiah. If Jesus had adopted this course of action, the people would never been satisfied. He would have had to produce greater and greater sensations to retain His power and popularity. Jesus would have no part of it. Again, quoting Scripture, Jesus reminded Satan, "Do not put the Lord your God to the test" (Matthew 4:7).

Satan's third approach was to tempt Jesus to ignore the commandment, "Thou shalt have no other gods before me" (Exodus 20:3 KJV). He "took Jesus to a very high mountain and showed him all the kingdoms of the world in all their greatness. 'All this I will give you,' the Devil said, 'if you fall down and worship me'" (Matthew 4:8–9).

As Jesus looked to the left and to the right, taking in the panoramic view before Him, He knew Satan was trying to get Him to compromise, to settle for an earthly kingdom instead of building a spiritual one. He must have felt this temptation acutely because He said, "Go away, Satan!" and then quoted

Scripture. He said, "Worship the Lord your God and serve only him!" (Matthew 4:10).

This duel with Satan took 40 days. The struggle was so spiritually taxing that God sent angels to minister to Him when it was over (Mark 1:13; Matthew 4:11). By the time the duel was over, the principles for Jesus' ministry were established.

- He would not bribe people into following Him.
- The way of sensationalism was not for Him.
- He would not compromise His message; He would not worship Satan.

Those principles would be challenged from time to time as Jesus completed His mission. He knew where He was headed and how He would handle it, but the drama of being the Messiah who would suffer and die still had to be played out on the stage of life. The struggle wasn't over.

The continuing struggle

I heard two Christian leaders discussing stress. They agreed that Jesus' life was one without stress. They said He had an unhurried, peaceful lifestyle. I couldn't help wondering if we had been reading the same Gospels, because Jesus' struggle wasn't over when the period of temptations ended (Luke 4:13). As the Cross loomed near, He said to His disciples, "Ye are they which have continued with me in my temptations" (Luke 22:28 KJV).

Although His ministry began in obscurity, within a year His popularity exploded. On various occasions He tried to withdraw from the crowds. Even when He attempted to go into Gentile territory where He thought He was not well known, people found Him (Mark 7:24). The needy were always seeking Him.

Jesus taught with authority and rebelled against the oral and scribal laws. The religious leaders constantly ridiculed Him. They tried to discredit Him or trap Him in front of people. He was chased out of His own hometown. He lost His welcome in the synagogues. Even His family didn't understand Him or His mission.

Jesus operated within a limited time frame, knowing His time was short and knowing He had much work to do. His close associates did not grasp the kind of kingdom He was trying to set up. When Peter tried to keep Jesus from taking the way of the Cross, Jesus said to him words similar to what He said to Satan in the wilderness, "Get away from me, Satan!" (Matthew 16:23).

In his later ministry Jesus was watched and hunted. Toward the end of His life He was falsely accused and experienced unfair trials. He was betrayed by a co-worker and deserted by His friends. And, of course, there was the fight of all fights with temptation that Jesus waged in Gethsemane when Satan sought to deflect Him from the Cross (Luke 22:42–44; Matthew 26:36–46; Mark 14:32–42).

Sounds stressful to me! Doing God's will was not a simple matter for Jesus.

The "also" factor

In addition to knowing that Jesus struggled, we must believe that He did if we are to identify with Him and learn how to pray about what we can't change. Giving mental assent to something is not the same as believing.

Jesus was human as well as divine. Many of us accept this statement on an intellectual level. In other words, if we were asked on a test if Jesus was both human and divine, we would know the answer was yes. In our hearts, though, we don't really believe it. We tend to believe that the divine, so evident in His life, kept Jesus free and lifted Him above the circumstances of life.

To assume that His divinity kept Him free of the struggles, the questionings, the fears, and the loneliness that are part of being human is to undermine the truth of the incarnation. He was human; the Word was made flesh (see John 1:14). He was made like us.

If we don't believe Jesus struggled—if we don't acknowledge His humanity—then we will miss an important point of connection with Him. We are more likely to imitate those with whom we feel a similarity or a kindred spirit. Identification leads to imitation.

We see this identification/imitation pattern in the Apostle Peter's words to suffering believers, "For even hereunto were ye called: because Christ also suffered for us, leaving us an example, that ye should follow his steps" (1 Peter 2:21 KJV).

Peter's use of the word *also* connects our suffering with Jesus'. It's a comfort to know that Jesus Himself went through experiences like ours. It makes us feel like we are in the struggle together.

The word Peter used for *example* is very vivid. As Kenneth Wuest explained in his word study of *First Peter in the Greek New Testament*,

> *The word means literally "writing under." It was used of words given children to copy. . . . Sometimes it was used with reference to the act of tracing over written letters. . . . Just as a child slowly, with painstaking effort and close application, follows the shape of the letters of his teacher.* [2]

So we should follow the example of Jesus. He is our template.

Then Peter switched from the idea of a child tracing over the teacher's writing to following the footprints left by Jesus. Just as a child follows the footprints of a parent or older sibling in the sand, Peter encourages us to follow the footprints of Jesus. As we follow, we imitate Him.

After her diving accident, it took Joni Eareckson Tada three years to connect with Jesus. Those years were filled with tears, bitterness, and violent questionings concerning her paralysis. In seconds, her life had changed from one of vigorous activity and independence to total helplessness and dependence. Philip Yancey, in his book *Where Is God When It Hurts?*, describes the moment Joni identified with Jesus.

> *Cindy, one of Joni's closest friends, was beside her bed, searching desperately for some way to encourage Joni. Finally, she clumsily blurted out, "Joni, Jesus knows how you feel—you aren't the only one—why, He was paralyzed too."*
>
> *Joni glared at her. "What? What are you talking about?"*
>
> *Cindy continued, "It's true. Remember He was nailed on a cross. His back was raw from beatings, and He must have yearned for a way to move to change positions, or redistribute His weight. But He couldn't. He was paralyzed by the nails."* [3]

Joni found the connection deeply comforting. Once she identified with Jesus, she could learn from Him how to deal with what she could not change. They were "in it together." Her focus changed from demanding an explanation from God to depending on Him and learning from Him.

Making the connection

Many of us hold in our minds the picture of Jesus praying in the Garden of Gethsemane that is displayed in many churches and included in many Bibles. It is the picture where a halo encircles Jesus' head and light streams down from above. He looks serene and calm, but it is not very real as we'll see when we get to the chapter on His praying in the garden.

If we only see Jesus in this way, with a halo and light streaming down at Him from above, He isn't someone we can identify with because we are ordinary people. We don't have halos. We think Jesus couldn't understand what we are going through; He certainly would never need to pray, but the gospels show us that He did. And I believe Jesus wanted us to know He needed to pray. Otherwise He wouldn't have been so open about honestly praying in front of other people, something He did frequently.

I believe He also wanted us to know He experienced struggle, otherwise we wouldn't have known about His wilderness temptations. Jesus had been alone—no watchful observers were with Him when this struggle occurred. No reporters or cameramen were recording the scene. The story could have come from nowhere else other than Jesus' own lips. Jesus Himself must have told His disciples about this experience during some moment of intimate conversation. In telling it, He laid bare His heart and His soul so that those of us like Lois and Joni—those of us who struggle with something we can't change—could connect with Him. Once connected, we can learn from Him, if we believe Jesus struggled and that He needed to pray.

From inspiration to application

In coping with what I can't change, who am I imitating?

What do Jesus and I have in common?

What is the difference between knowing Jesus struggled and believing He did?

"Lord, I believe; help thou mine unbelief." [4]

Part II

The Solution
Walking with Jesus

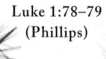

*"Because the heart of our God is full of mercy
toward us, the first light of Heaven shall come
to visit us—to shine on those who lie in darkness
and under the shadow of death,
and to guide our feet into
the path of peace."*

**Luke 1:78–79
(Phillips)**

Chapter 4

Going or Staying?

"The little town said to Jesus 'Stay.' The little road said, 'Go.' He said, 'Let us go.' There is a very real sense in which, if we have the mind of Christ and have caught his spirit, we must 'go on to the next towns.' We must go on to the next stage in our religious experience."[1]

Halford E. Luccock

D o you remember the phone call we've been waiting for, the one that would tell us the cross for the top of our church had arrived?" asked the pastor. "Well, the call came Friday night."

Murmurs and chuckles rippled through the congregation. On Friday night, it had snowed.

"It had been snowing a couple of hours and darkness was settling in when I received the call. The truck driver said, 'I have your cross. I must quickly unload it and be on my way. Where is the church?'

"I told him our church was located north of town right off the main highway. I said, 'You'll easily spot it because it sits on top of a high hill. I'll meet you at the bottom of the hill.'

"When I arrived, I got into the cab with the driver. He tried to drive the truck up the hill, but the fresh snow made the steep hill too slick. We talked about what to do and decided to carry the cross.

"I carried the small box of attachments and the truck driver carried the cross. It was as tall as he was, and he hoisted it over his shoulder. It was snowing too hard to make conversation, so we walked in silence. In the fading daylight, I watched the driver ahead of me slip and stumble with the bulky cross. Immediately, my thoughts turned to Jesus and His walk to Calvary. I'll admit I had never really thought about what that walk must have been like for Him, but I thought a lot about it Friday night. I had a new appreciation for what he went through."

As the pastor went on talking, I thought, *I wish I could have an experience like that.*[2] I had a hunch that something dramatic, something where I could actually put myself in Jesus' place for a while, would draw me closer to Him. Like the Apostle Paul, I wanted "to *know* Christ and the power of his resurrection and the fellowship of sharing in his sufferings" (Philippians 3:10 NIV; emphasis added).

Paul's aim wasn't to know about Christ. Paul had been a believer for many years when he expressed this desire. Paul's aim was to progressively become more deeply and intimately acquainted with Jesus. The pastor's story helped me to realize that I wanted the same thing.

Once I recognized this, I should have immediately pursued ways to know Jesus better, but I didn't. Like many good sermon listeners, my motivation disappeared once I left the church.

Maybe it was because I was still living in the anything-can-be-changed stage of life. Later, when I was discovering that everything in life can't be changed, I took hold of Jesus' hand and began walking with Him as I studied His prayer life. Where did He pray? When did He pray? What led Him to pray? What were His requests? How did He phrase them? Finding the answers to these questions helped me know Jesus more intimately.

Examining anyone's prayer life is hard. How can we really be certain about the thought processes of another individual, even a contemporary, even a loved one? Entering the mind of someone who lived 2,000 years ago and who was both God and man is even more difficult. Walking with Jesus takes effort.

Some analysis required

Where Jesus' actual prayers are recorded in the Bible, we know exactly what He prayed for. At other times, though, the object of His prayer is not stated; it is inferred by the circumstances. Here our judgment must enter in. We'll determine the object of prayer by looking at the actual incident, what happened before and what happened afterwards. This is how I determined what Jesus prayed about at His baptism (chap. 2).[3] Now let's see how this process of inference works in Mark 1:35, the first recorded incident of Jesus' praying after His baptism and His temptations in the wilderness.[4]

What happened before Jesus prayed. The first year of Jesus' ministry was mostly spent in Judea where John the Baptist preached and baptized. After John was put in prison, Jesus went to Galilee and preached the good news in Capernaum. While there, several events close together caused His popularity to explode.

- In the synagogue on the Sabbath, Jesus amazed the people by the way He taught. He wasn't like the scribes who quoted others; Jesus "taught with authority" (Mark 1:22).
- "Then a man with an evil spirit came into the synagogue" and screamed at Jesus (v. 23). Jesus ordered the evil spirit to come out of the man, and it did. The people were dumbfounded, "This man has authority to give orders to the evil spirits, and they obey him!" (v. 27). The presence of unclean spirits or demons was pervasive in their world so they were used to exorcists. The exorcists had various ways of casting out demons, but Jesus did it with a direct order. Amazing!
- News about Jesus and His ability spread quickly (v. 28).
- Jesus healed Simon Peter's mother-in-law (v. 31), and you can imagine what that did. By sundown, "people brought to Jesus all the sick and those who had demons. All the people of the town gathered in front of the house" (vv. 32–33) of Simon Peter and Andrew.

The incident of prayer. The morning after this intense day full of interaction with people and meeting needs, Jesus got up very early, long before daylight, and left the house. He went out of town to a solitary place where He prayed. The time and the place indicate a deliberate effort on the part of Jesus to get away from the crowds to be alone and to pray. He wanted to avoid people and other distractions; He wanted to communicate with the Father.

What happened after Jesus prayed. When Simon Peter and those with him awoke, they discovered that Jesus had disappeared. They went searching for Him. When they spotted

Jesus, they said, "Everyone is looking for you? (v. 37). "When they found him, they tried to keep him from leaving" (Luke 4:42). The multitude wanted to keep Him in their place, concerned about their locality only.

Jesus said that He must go on to the other villages. "I have to preach in them also, because that is why I came" (Mark 1:38).

The inference

When we pull together the press of the crowd, the escape to a solitary place, and Jesus' decision to leave, the inference is that Jesus prayed because He needed God's guidance.

Should He go or should He stay? The people of Capernaum were needy people; should He localize His ministry and stay there? It was a bustling city of many people. Wouldn't that be a large enough ministry area? Or should He go to other areas?

The disciples, too, might prefer that they stay where they were being successful. They were probably thrilled to see so many people come to Jesus. A ministry in one place would certainly be better for them.

Were numerous healings consistent with His mission? Jesus' popularity in Capernaum was due largely to the miracles He produced—driving out demons and healing many with various diseases. To be sure, miracles authenticated who He was and His message, but was healing to be His goal and main emphasis? Certainly, this would have pleased the people. Were they interested only in His miracles? If He stayed, would He be able to lead them on to deeper spiritual truths?

What did God want Him to do? The main question for Jesus was this one. While He knew His broad purpose and principles through His baptism and His temptations, He continued to need God's guidance about the specifics.

If that were not the case, Jesus would have been a mere robot or a puppet. He was a thinking person, a person who could be tempted, a person who interacted with people and responded to their needs; therefore, He needed to continually consult God.

Through prayer, Jesus came to understand what the specifics were at this time. He understood that He must leave the miracle-seeking multitude and go to other places. By the time Simon Peter and the others arrived, Jesus had his answer. He said, "I must preach the Good News of the Kingdom of God in other towns also, because that is what God sent me to do'" (Luke 4:43). He could say decisively and firmly what He was going to do because He had prayed.

Making the connection

Caitlin (from chap. 1) knew just enough about holiness to resist it. When God spoke to her at the student retreat, her initial response was, *Oh God, please don't ask me to change.* Resigning herself to what she figured was inevitable (God always has His way, doesn't He?), Caitlin verbally committed herself to changing her lifestyle in the retreat's closing commitment service.

On the ride back to campus, Caitlin realized she didn't know much about holiness. She knew the basic concept was one of separateness. Did that mean she would have to separate herself from all her non-Christian friends? Would she have to dress differently? Change her vocabulary? Change her habits? Would she be lonely? Would she be peculiar? Overwhelmed by the possibilities, Caitlin buried her face in her hands. She thought, *What have I gotten myself into? I'll never be able to live a holy life.*

Caitlin needed specifics about doing God's will just as Jesus did. To receive guidance, she had to be just as deliberate as He was.

Back at the dormitory, Caitlin set her alarm for 5:00 A. M. When the alarm went off the next morning, she reluctantly crawled out of her warm bed. Careful not to disturb her roommate, she grabbed her Bible and blanket and slipped out of her room. In the lounge, while other students were sleeping, Caitlin opened God's Word and opened her heart to discovering how He wanted her to live.

Morning after morning she continued this pattern. Many a morning Caitlin wanted to pull the covers close and avoid the loneliness of the lounge at 5:00 A.M. Yet on those mornings she thought of Jesus. She wondered if it had been hard for Him to leave Capernaum while everyone else was asleep. When she had been up really late studying for a test the night before, she wondered about Jesus' exhaustion from His busy day in Capernaum. Had it been hard for Him to get up long before daylight when His body was tired from the previous day's activities?

Thinking of Jesus gave Caitlin the determination and inspiration she needed to meet God for guidance in that lounge at the end of the hall. And in those moments, God spoke to her and showed her what He wanted. She received the guidance she needed—and more.

- God strengthened Caitlin's resolve to be different; He gave her the courage to be His person.
- At first she looked upon God's call to holiness as bondage, but as she disciplined herself to be like Jesus, she experienced freedom. Now, she could be her authentic self instead of being a chameleon trying to please everyone.

- She grew closer to Jesus. He had been her Savior ever since she became a Christian as a child, but now He was also her friend.
- She experienced spiritual power. As she took on the nature of Jesus, she began to see others through His eyes. She now saw her sophisticated friends as spiritually needy, and she reached out to help them instead of trying to impress them.

When Caitlin looks back on the guidance, freedom, intimacy, and power she discovered from identifying with and imitating Jesus, she wonders why she ever bristled at living by God's unchangeable standards.

Maybe the work involved had something to do with it. To walk with Jesus, to identify with Him and to imitate Him requires effort. Examining His prayer life even requires effort because we must pull together and analyze information.

Motivation may also have something to do with it. Some of us aren't motivated to walk with Jesus until we come up against something we can't change. I wasn't the day I left the church with the new steeple. You may not be at that place either; your options are still wide open. No matter where we find ourselves, Jesus extends the invitation to us, "Follow Me." The questions before us are, *Will we go or will we stay? Will we go forward to seek to know Him more fully or will we stay where we are?*

From inspiration to application

What kind of mental work is necessary to understanding Jesus' prayers?

How can I become more deeply and intimately acquainted with Jesus?

What is one way I can discover the specifics of doing God's will?

"In the morning, O Lord, you hear my voice;
In the morning I lay my requests before you
and wait in expectation." [5]

Chapter 5

Seeking Help in Lonely Places

"We who live in the quiet places have the opportunity to become acquainted with ourselves, to think our own thoughts and live our own lives in a way that is not possible for those who are keeping up with the crowd."[1]

Laura Ingalls Wilder

When Jesus was in Capernaum, the place where His popularity exploded, people brought their sick and demon possessed to be healed. No mention was made of anyone being healed of leprosy (Mark 1:32, 34). Perhaps it is implied in "healed many who were ill with various diseases" (v. 34 NASB), but maybe not. People probably wouldn't have gathered up their leprous family members and brought them to Jesus because they were terrified of the horribly disfiguring disease. Leprosy was thought to be highly contagious so once a diagnosis was made, a leper was banished from society. They were untouchables.

Word, though, about Jesus' phenomenal works must have reached a leper's ears, giving him hope and determination.

He went looking for Jesus. "When he saw Jesus, he fell with his face to the ground and begged him, 'Lord, if you are willing, you can make me clean'" (Luke 5:12 NIV). It was a request that would influence both of their lives.

The leper's life-changing encounter

After Jesus left Capernaum, He preached and healed in other Galilean cities, and it was in one of those towns that the leper approached Him. The leper approached Jesus hoping against hope that he could be healed; he had heard enough about Jesus to know it was possible. In desperation, he begged Jesus to heal him. It would mean everything to him to be healed and to be able to rejoin society. He knew Jesus could do it, but would He? Would He want to heal someone like him, somebody society rejected? The leper said to Jesus, "Sir, if you want to, you can make me clean!" (Luke 5:12).

And then in a way that touches my heart every time I read it, Jesus healed the man. "Jesus reached out and touched him. 'I do want to,' he said. 'Be clean!'" (v. 13).

Jesus touched the man; He didn't need to do this to heal him. He could have healed the leper without touching him; He did in other cases. I can only imagine what this touch meant to someone who had been declared untouchable, and then what was even more beautiful were Jesus' words. He said, "I want to. Be clean!"

Immediately the leprosy left the man. He was healed, he could reenter society, go back home to his family, and pick up where life had left off! First, though, there was something he had to do.

"Jesus ordered him, 'Don't tell anyone, but go straight to the priest and let him examine you; then to prove to everyone that you are cured, offer the sacrifice as Moses ordered'"

(v. 14). It is understandable that Jesus told him to go to the priest and to offer sacrifice. If he showed the priest evidence of his healing, made an offering of thanksgiving, cleansed his body, and changed his clothes, he could become an accepted part of society again.

What is harder to understand is Jesus saying, "Don't tell anyone." That's sounds like an odd request. Why wouldn't Jesus want everyone to know He healed a serious case of leprosy? Wouldn't that get Him even more followers? Wouldn't that reveal even more of His power? What would telling this story mean for Jesus?

What a story could do

Once told, this story would accent how powerful and daring Jesus was. This combination would prompt the people to pressure Jesus into becoming their leader.

The people were already aware that Jesus could heal, but leprosy? It was an incurable disease, and this man had a serious case. The Bible describes him as "covered with leprosy" (v. 12 NIV) or "full of leprosy" (v. 12 NASB). If they knew He could heal leprosy, He would be even more spectacular in the eyes of the people. They would expect more and more from Jesus because of the power He revealed. They hadn't known anyone who had had healed a serious case of leprosy!

When Jesus healed the leper, He had defied Jewish law. The law said you must not touch a leper. This raised eyebrows and so did Jesus' saying to the leper, "Be clean." Only the priest in the temple in Jerusalem was supposed to declare a leper clean. This defilement raised criticism but it also raised people's appreciation. Jesus was courageous and daring.

Observing His power and His courage, the people might see in Him their Rescuer. The Jews were subservient to the Romans who were in power. They dreamed of a day when a divine deliverer would come. This deliverance would be in terms of military conquest and political power. For this to be possible, a strong, powerful, daring leader would be needed.

If the cured leper told his story, it would increase Jesus' popularity. The people might want to install Jesus as their political leader and military commander, and that wasn't Jesus' mission. Jesus had to help them "to see that His power was love and not force of arms. He had to work almost in secrecy until men knew Him for what He was, the lover and not the destroyer of the lives of men." [2]

The healed leper, though, had no idea of what the ramifications for Jesus would be if he told his story. He ignored Jesus' instructions to not tell. He "began to talk freely, spreading the news" (Mark 1:45 NIV). Consequently, "the news about Jesus spread all the more widely, and crowds of people came to hear him and be healed from their diseases" (Luke 5:15).

The need for lonely places

The spreading of the story of the leper's healing increased Jesus' popularity, taking it to a new level. It wasn't a crowd anymore who gathered to hear Him and be healed of their diseases, it was "crowds." Great multitudes gathered to hear Him and to be healed of their sicknesses. "*But* he would go away to lonely places, where he prayed" (Luke 5:16; author's italics).

Jesus deliberately left the crowds which included needy people to pray. He sought out lonely places to do this. While we've already seen Him do this on two other occasions— and we'll see more as we move along—there must have been many other occasions in which He did this. As the New

International Version translates this verse, it says "Jesus *often* withdrew to lonely places and prayed" (Luke 5:16; author's italics). Where did He go?

- "Into the desert" (Matthew 4:1; Mark 1:12; Luke 4:1) or "the wilderness" (KJV). These were uninhabited regions.
- "Out of town to a lonely place" (Mark 1:35) or "a solitary place" (KJV).
- "The wilderness" (Luke 5:16 KJV) or "to lonely places."
- "Up a hill" (Luke 6:12) or "out into a mountain" (KJV).
- "Departed into a mountain to pray" (Mark 6:46 KJV), "to a hill to pray," or "up on a mountainside" (NIV).
- "Into a deserted place by ship privately" (Mark 6:32 KJV) or "by themselves to a lonely place."
- "Left there in a boat and went to a lonely place" (Matthew 14:13) or "into a deserted place" (KJV).

The places varied, but they all are places where He could be alone. They were all places where He could experience solitude and pray. Why would Jesus make withdrawal a regular part of His prayer life? Why did He need lonely places to pray? And why might we need to imitate His practice?

The benefits of lonely places

What did prayerful solitude do for Jesus, and what can it do for those of us who are trying to come to grips with what we can't change?

Solitude offers privacy for dealing with emotions. When Jesus heard the news about the martyrdom of John the Baptist, He left the crowd and went by boat to a lonely place (Matthew 14:13). Through John's ministry Jesus had been baptized and had received direction for His own work in the world. John's death was a sobering reminder to Jesus that He, too, would suffer a similar fate. Facing His grief over the loss of a ministry colleague and the realization of the danger He was facing called for solitude.

Emotions accompany things we can't change (something we'll talk more about later as we continue to walk with Jesus). Some of those emotions can be very strong—too strong to share even with friends. Or we may be conscious that others are watching us, waiting to see how we are going to respond. We don't need this kind of scrutinizing when we are struggling to make adjustments. Solitude gives us a place to deal with our emotions apart from watchful eyes and where we can be free to express them.

In his book *A Grace Disguised*, Gerald L. Sittser, a college teacher who lost his mother, his wife, and a daughter in an automobile accident, described how solitude helped him to handle his loss. His moments of solitude were late in the evening, after his remaining children were in bed. He writes,

> *Sometimes I listened to music—mostly requiems, Gregorian chants, and other choral works; and sometimes I wrote in my journal or read good books. But mostly I sat in my rocking chair and stared into space, reliving the accident and remembering the people I lost. I felt anguish in my soul and cried bitter tears.[3]*

He said that this nightly solitude became sacred to him "because it allowed time for genuine mourning and intense reflection."[4]

Solitude facilitates thinking. Jesus needed a lonely place, without the presence of people and their continual interruptions, to sort out His thoughts and to seek God's guidance. He cared about the people who flocked to see Him; He was concerned about the people who needed healing, but is this where God wanted Him to place His emphasis? Was this going to show people what God was like and what He desired for them? Would He be able to resist the pressure to be a political messiah instead of a spiritual savior?

When we struggle with something we can't change, we may be bombarded by swirling thoughts. The thoughts and their intensity will vary depending on the individual and what can't be changed. Solitude provides a climate for sorting out those thoughts.

When Peggy (from chap. 1) was diagnosed with scleroderma, she was so dismayed by the diagnosis that she thought about taking her life. She wondered what effects the illness would have on her children and her husband, and she wondered what God's will for her was.

Even though Peggy had a regular quiet time of prayer and Bible study, those moments weren't long enough to sort out her questions. She worked full time and was concerned about being late for work. She needed unhurried time but couldn't find that because her family was planning a major long-distance move.

Peggy said, "When we moved, I knew I wouldn't have to work outside the home for a while. I promised myself . . . I'd take the time to really work through this disease thing with God."

Peggy used the lonely days following their move—when she wasn't interrupted by phone calls or activities and when her life was not highly scheduled—to sort out her thoughts and to seek God's guidance.

When we leave the crowded city and head for a nature preserve, when we climb a mountain and change our view, when we escape the noises of radios and televisions, when we turn off our cell phones, and stop looking for text messages, our breathing slows, our heart stops beating so rapidly, and our thinking improves. This may take awhile as we separate ourselves from the things and people that consume our attention. Apart from distractions, we have a keener quality of attention that helps us examine alternatives and find solutions.

Solitude improves listening. Once we sort out our thoughts, we need God's guidance on how to proceed. That requires communication.

Jesus' rising before dawn to pray and His spending nights in prayer implies that communion with God frequently requires unhurried quiet. Communion with God requires dialogue—speaking, listening, waiting, and receiving. While this can be done in the presence of distractions, it is easier to listen and to receive when we are not distracted and when we are not in a hurry.

David Hazard, the editor of a devotional series drawn from classic Christian writings, writes, "Throughout Scripture and church history, God has always shown up and spoken His mind whenever humans have taken seriously His call to quiet."[5] In a lonely place, unhurried by the demands of people, by our schedules or by our technology, our receptivity for hearing God's voice is heightened.

Solitude refreshes. Once Jesus became popular in Galilee, He was rarely without a crowd around Him.

- When He was on His way to Jairus's house, so many people were going along with Jesus that they crowded Him from every side (Mark 5:24).
- He was forced to preach from a borrowed boat in order to distance Himself from the growing crowd on the shore (Matthew 13:2).
- The paralytic's friends lowered him through a hole in the

roof because of the crowd surrounding Jesus (Mark 2:4).

- When the apostles returned from their missions assignment, they tried to tell Jesus about it, but so many people were coming and going that they didn't even have time to eat (Mark 6:31). As the people clamored around them, Jesus said, "Come away by yourselves to a lonely place and rest a while" (Mark 6:31 NASB).
- When Jesus tried to retreat with the apostles for training and rest, He didn't want anyone to know where they were, but Jesus could not be hidden (Mark 7:24).

The demands upon Jesus' sympathy and compassion were unrelenting. To continue to respond to the many pressing needs around Him was emotionally and spiritually draining. When Jesus healed someone, it took something out of Him. Matthew, in quoting Isaiah, said of Jesus, "He took up our infirmities and carried our diseases" (Matthew 8:17 NIV). When the woman with the hemorrhage of blood touched Jesus, He said, "I was aware that power had gone out of Me" (Luke 8:46 NASB). *The Interpreter's Bible* states, "In order that he might respond to the pitiful thirst for help of those who flocked to him, he had to separate himself from time to time that through communion with his Father the reservoirs of his own soul might be filled again from the fountains that were on high."[6] Or as we might say, you can't always be giving out unless you are sometimes taking in.

When we seek out the lonely places, when we commune with God while there, we give Him the opportunity to renew our resources. Sittser, who struggled with exhaustion, said that his nighttime solitude gave him freedom during the day to invest his energy into his work and into caring for his children.

When we seek the lonely places, we have an opportune place and time to let our emotions surface, to sort out our thoughts, to really listen to God, and to be refreshed by Him. With so many benefits, you would think we would all be eager to seek out lonely places, but yet some of us hesitate. Why is that?

Avoiding lonely places

Despite the benefits of solitary time with God, some of us may be reluctant to visit lonely places. We hesitate for a variety of reasons.

- We may be so hurt over what has happened to us—what it is that we can't change—that we want to avoid God. We don't want to hear His voice. We may not say this out loud, but in our heart, we fault Him for what happened so we don't want to be in His presence.
- We may not want to acknowledge our emotions. We may pride ourselves on being unemotional, or we may be afraid of expressing emotions. Releasing grief and anger can be unpleasant and even agonizing.
- We may be afraid the solitude will be painful, and it may be, particularly at first. It may feel like you are entering a place of darkness at first instead of a place of light.
- We may be on a treadmill of nonstop activity, and we cannot see how we can get off, even if it is for just a day, or two, or a few hours. Faxes are coming in, mail is arriving, the phone is ringing, email messages are piling up. If we take time out, we will get behind.
- Perhaps we feel that to seek solitude is to face

being alone, something that petrifies us, so we surround ourselves with noise and people. We simply can't face time alone.

- We may insist we have no place to be alone. Our space is crowded. Someone is always around.
- While we acknowledge that solitude helped Jesus, we may think, It really wouldn't help me. Yet that's exactly what Satan would have us think. He would like for us to miss out on the benefits of solitude.

There could be other reasons, but the point is: we may have to be just as deliberate and persevering as Jesus was to reap the benefits of solitude. The people who pursued Him were very aggressive. They seemed to have an uncanny sense for knowing where He was and how to find Him. They were ever present with their many needs—needs I'm sure Jesus didn't want to ignore; although at times, He did. We may have to be just as deliberate to sort out our thoughts and feelings, to commune with God and to give Him a channel to guide us and refresh us. The results will be worth the effort.

From inspiration to application

As I deal with what I can't change, what thoughts are circulating in my head? What feelings do I have? How could solitude help me deal with either?

Where are some lonely places I can use to commune with God?

What is preventing me from visiting those places?

"Silently now I wait for Thee,
Ready, my God, Thy will to see." [7]

Chapter 6

What Do I Do Now?

"Painful as it may be, a significant emotional event can be the catalyst for choosing a direction that serves us—and those around us—more effectively."[1]

Louisa May Alcott

When Mark, whom you met in chapters 1 and 2, told his wife, Susan, that he was fired from his position of area sales representative for a major book publisher, she asked, "What are we going to do now?" What she really wanted to know was, *What are we going to live on? What kind of financial resources do we have? And how can we best use them?*

Allan, whom you also met in chapter 1, had to make quick choices when Ruth died so unexpectedly. He chose the type of funeral and where she would be buried. With his daughters, they decided what to do with Ruth's belongings. After his daughters had returned to their homes, Allan had tougher choices to make: *How do I live without Ruth? How do I redefine myself as a single person?*

Mark's and Allan's situations remind us that choices accompany things we can't change. That combination sounds incongruous, doesn't it? Choice and "can't" don't seem to go together—but they do. If we look closely, we'll see that with most unchangeables comes a choice or choices. We will have decisions to make. What can we learn from Jesus that will help us in making critical decisions?

A developing need

When Jesus heard God's voice at His baptism, He knew He was God's chosen Messiah. He knew the way for Him was the way of the Cross. While He could not change that destiny, He had many decisions to make as He interpreted what it meant to be the Messiah.

The task of being the Messiah included showing what God really wanted in the way of worship and obedience. Religion for many Jews had become a matter of rules and regulations. Jesus openly rebelled, and naturally opposition followed.

At the heart of the opposition was Jesus' disregard for the Sabbath rules and regulations. Honoring the seventh day of the week by not working had developed into a very complicated and burdensome responsibility. Moses' instructions had been elaborated and multiplied until they numbered in the hundreds. These were oral restrictions—the written ones didn't change—that made the keeping of the Sabbath practically impossible. What's worse, keeping the oral law destroyed the spirit of the Sabbath.

Jesus could not tolerate the numerous and ridiculous regulations. He wanted people to truly know God and not have their faith stifled in the observance of these regulations. Jesus openly challenged the system, even healing a man whose condition could have waited until another day.

Jesus left Galilee temporarily to attend the Passover in Jerusalem. While He was there, He healed a lame man on the Sabbath (John 5:1–18). This man's life was not in danger; Jesus could have waited until Monday or Tuesday to heal him, but He wanted to make a point about the Sabbath.

On the way back to Galilee (Mark 2:23–28; Matthew 12:1–8; and Luke 6:1–5), Jesus and His disciples passed a wheat field. The disciples plucked some heads of wheat, rubbed them in their hands to remove the chaff, and ate them. While this was permissible according to the law of Moses (Deuteronomy 23:25), it was a violation of the rules regarding the Sabbath in the oral law. "So the Pharisees said to Jesus, 'Look, it is against our law for your disciples to do that on the Sabbath!'" (Mark 2:24).

Back in Galilee (Mark 3:1–6; Matthew 12:9–12; and Luke 6:6–11), in the synagogue on the Sabbath, Jesus healed a man with a withered hand—another healing that could have waited if He had not wanted to be controversial. Luke said the religious leaders were "filled with rage" because Jesus had healed a man on the Sabbath (6:11). They entered in what was for them an unholy alliance with a secular group called the Herodians. Together they made plans to kill Jesus (Mark 3:6). The intensity of the opposition reminded Jesus that time was running out.

The crucial choice

There was so much Jesus wanted to say, to teach, and to do. He wanted the people to know what God really wanted and what He was like. Jesus wanted to make sure His message continued after His death.

If only He could reach people in more places, but He could only be in one place at a time. His voice could reach only a limited number of people. In that day there were no means of mass communication. There was no Internet. If any message was presented to people, it was presented personally.

If Jesus' work was to branch out—and go on—Jesus needed helpers to accompany Him, to strengthen His ministry (Mark 3:14b). He needed preachers (v. 14c) to spread His message and to guarantee its existence after He was gone. At this time of crisis, Jesus "went up a hill to pray and spent the whole night there praying to God. When day came, he called his disciples to him, and chose twelve of them, whom he named apostles" (Luke 6:12–13).

Though this passage doesn't state in so many words the purpose for this deliberate, all-night prayer vigil, the inference is there. Most Bible commentators unite in recognizing that it was in some manner associated with choosing the 12 apostles. The choice of who those men would be was so crucial that "he went off to the mountain to pray, and He spent the whole night in prayer to God" (v. 12 NASB).

The place of decision

Climbing a mountain or hill, taking in the view from the heights facilitates a spiritual experience. Climbing, going from a lower level to a higher level, helps us to disengage ourselves from problems and gives us a clearer mind to communicate with God. The view from the mountaintop facilitates a person's ability to gain God's perspective. In Jesus' case, spending the night on the mountain might have aided His communion with God. As the sun went down and the stars came out, He may have felt closer to God and have been reminded of God's power. The mountain gave Him a place apart from distractions, so He could fully concentrate on communing with God about the decision He needed to make.

Jesus took the trouble to climb the mountain specifically to pray. Jesus did not go out for a hike up the mountain and then decide it would be nice to pray. His climbing a mountain reflected the urgency of the burden He carried and His desire for perspective—God's perspective. It would take all night to express thoughts and to gain God's view. Alone and apart from all the distractions of the world below, Jesus sought illumination and guidance.

The time involved

This choice was so crucial that Jesus spent the "whole night" in prayer. The Greek word translated "whole night" is a medical term. It was used to describe the all-night vigil of a doctor as he waited at the bedside of a patient. The original word presents a picture of intense urgency and earnestness. This reminds us of the work involved in prayer. It looks like a very simple, "God, what would you have me to do" would be answered immediately, but frequently it takes dialogue, verbalization, waiting, and listening to receive God's answer.

As He considered the urgency of His need, I'm sure part of His prayer work was weighing the alternatives before Him. Because we know He chose Simon Peter, Andrew, James, John, Philip, Bartholomew, Matthew, Thomas, James the son of Alphaeus, Simon the Zealot, Judas the son of James, and Judas Iscariot, we don't usually think about Jesus having alternatives, but He did. Many consider the number He chose to be symbolic, linking the apostles to the 12 tribes of Israel, connecting Jesus as the Messiah with a reconstituted Israel. But even that concept had to come to Jesus. Had He considered other possibilities? Maybe He considered seven because it was the perfect number or because a smaller group would have been easier to travel with?

Somewhere in that long prayer vigil, when the concept of the Twelve came to him, the next question was, who would the Twelve be? Out of all His disciples, who would be willing to identify their life with His? The crowds might be there one day and gone the next. Followers might fluctuate and be spasmodic in their attachment to Jesus, but He needed helpers who were dependable. Which ones would be faithful over the long haul? Who would be willing to travel and to be homeless? Which ones were courageous enough to identify with a rebel? Jesus was branded a sinner and a heretic; the opposition was determined to get Him. They would have to be courageous just to travel with Him.

As Jesus pondered the alternatives and their consequences, He listened. This is one reason why we need time when we seek God's will—so we can hear God responding, leading us along, directing our thinking, illuminating the situation, and bringing new thoughts to our mind. Indeed, Elton Trueblood once referred to this activity as "the white heat of prayer."[2] In this environment, "ideas fuse to form new unities, when they cannot fuse in colder environments."[3] In a vigil of prayer, we give God a warm environment for illuminating our choice and guiding us.

By morning He had His answer. He called His disciples to Him and chose 12 men from among them to be apostles. He chose them to strengthen His ministry and to see that it continued after His death. Through prayer Jesus made a choice that enabled His ministry to expand beyond the limitations of space and time.

With some choices that accompany what we can't change, we will need to maintain a vigil of prayer just as Jesus did. Decisions that are crucial, involving far-reaching consequences, may need hours of prayer to discover God's will. Maintaining a vigil doesn't necessarily mean spending one night in prayer, but it does mean spending time in prayer. We will need time to identify our choices, look at the alternatives, consider their consequences and most importantly, listen for God's answer.

Identifying our choices

Leah had urgent choices to make when her husband was killed in a freak hunting accident. At the time, Leah was a stay-at-home pastor's wife with two small children. Her husband's death meant the loss of their income and the parsonage they had lived in for four years. In one blow, she lost her husband, her income, and her home. While trying to come to grips with her husband's death, Leah had to figure out where she and the children were going to live and how they were going to pay for it. She had to make choices about a job, about child care, and about housing.

Sometimes the choices that accompany what we can't change will not be as obvious as Leah's. They won't have urgency to them like the need for money, shelter, child care, etc. They may be more nebulous choices, such as:

- Will I accept or reject what I cannot change?
- Will I define what happened as the end or a new beginning?
- Will I hold on to the person I was, or will I grow with the experience?

The impact of what we can't change may leave us feeling like we have no choices. Or we may get bogged down emotionally. Our grief, resentment, anger, or despair may blind us to our choices. Some confession may be needed. We may need to pray, "Father, I feel trapped and I feel cheated. Open my eyes to possibilities. Help me to see the choices I have."

Identifying our choices is important. The power to choose gives us the ability to transcend our circumstances and to grow and to gain from them. Otherwise we may begin to see ourselves as victims and remain stuck in the mire of what we cannot change.

Looking at alternatives

What Leah really wanted was to go back to the way life was when her husband was alive, but she couldn't. People kept asking her, "What are you going to do? Where are you going to go?" Then the church trustees told her she needed to be out of the parsonage in six months. While they were kind in how they said it, and Leah understood their need for a time limit, she felt an increasing sense of doom. She had to make choices whether she wanted to or not.

Because of her small children, Leah couldn't withdraw "to the hills" for an overnight prayer vigil. She could, though, get up early before her children were awake. In the early morning quiet, she verbalized her needs for housing, for a job, and for child care. Taking a pencil and paper, she listed various alternatives as they came to her. Just seeing the alternatives lifted her spirits. She felt a little more hopeful about her future.

The next morning she gathered more strength as she prayed over each alternative. She eliminated some and added others. Morning by morning she prayerfully pared the list down to those that seemed reasonable and appropriate.

Considering the consequences

Each alternative and its consequences need to be carefully considered. What's going to happen if I follow alternative A? What's going to be the result if I were to go in B direction? This exercise may be something we're tempted to overlook or to avoid. It's just too analytical for praying, but I think it is important to think things through. If we don't weigh the consequences of our choices, we may end up surprised at God's answer. We might even be tempted to be angry with Him, and here's why.

Sometimes in the emotional turmoil of struggling with something we can't change, we long for a perfect answer to prayer—an answer that spells end of struggle. If the answer we receive involves more struggle, we may become angry. More growth is the last thing we want! Comfort or a final solution is what we have in mind when we pray.

God is trustworthy, so we don't have to be afraid of His answers, but we may be surprised by them. The men God led Jesus to choose had all kinds of faults. Some of them were given to emotional outbursts. Some argued about positions of honor. One denied knowing Jesus, and another betrayed him. God's answer did not spell end of struggle for Jesus, but God's answer was sufficient. These ordinary men, with their faults, strengthened Jesus' ministry. Through them, Jesus' message survived, as the Book of Acts reveals.

Listening to God

As He considered the urgency of His need, as He looked at the alternatives before Him, as He considered their consequences, He listened. Listening is the most important element in the choice-making prayer vigil. It is in listening that we receive God's answer. It's a moment worth waiting for, because then we can proceed with confidence.

Some of Leah's friends grew impatient with her when she didn't take the jobs that became available in their community. But Leah knew they weren't the jobs God had for her. In her early-morning prayer vigil, God showed her the kind of job she needed, so she held out for that kind of job. She found it two weeks before she was to be out of the parsonage.

I don't understand why a vigil is sometimes required to receive God's answer. It looks like, if our hearts are sincere, we could just ask God what to do, and He would tell us. On occasion we may actually receive His instructions that easily, but more often the process takes time. It's almost as if the process itself is important. Maybe it is. As we pray, we unfold ourselves, opening our will to His leadership. We sift and weigh, changing our perspective to match God's perspective. Our vision widens; our hope rises. We pray on, listening until the moment comes when we know we have God's answer.

From inspiration to application

What kind of environment (place) would help me with praying about what I can't change?

What choice or choices do I have regarding what I can't change?

What are the corresponding alternatives?

What are the consequences of each alternative?

How will I know when I have God's answer about what I should do?

"Lord, what wilt thou have me to do?" [4]

Chapter 7

Being Faithful Regardless

"Weapons which the Christian can use ... are *steadfastness* and loyalty. The word for steadfastness is that great word *hupomone*, which does not simply mean passively bearing things; it means courageously accepting the worst that life can do, and turning it into glory. The word for loyalty is *pistis*, and it means that fidelity which will never waver in its utter devotion to its Master and its Lord."[1]

William Barclay

When my children were small, I often read to them *Tootle* a little book by Gertrude Crampton. Tootle was a small locomotive. He attended a school for locomotives so he could become the Flyer train between New York and Chicago. Tootle could never be a good train, let alone the Flyer, unless he made an A+ in the course called, Staying on the Rails No Matter What.

One day while Tootle was practicing staying on the rails, a strong black horse came running across the meadow. "Race you to the river!" he shouted. Tootle accepted the challenge, left the track, and raced the horse through the meadow. Once Tootle discovered how nice it was in the meadow, he was easily distracted by buttercups, a frog, and daisies.

As my children wondered how Tootle was ever going to learn to stay on the rails, I thought of how Christians have to learn the same lesson. We are often tempted to get off the narrow "way, which leadeth unto life" (Matthew 7:14 KJV). This may be especially true when we are dealing with things we can't change.

We may look at others whose lives appear easier than ours. How come they seem to be exempt from heartache? Am I on the wrong track?

Life may seem to be too hard. We get weary of trying to live right, deal with resistance, adjust to our circumstances and try to keep going. Wouldn't it be easier to bail out?

God may not have acted in accordance with what we believe. As we study the Bible, as we read what others write, and as we listen to what others say, we develop assumptions about God. When God does something not in accordance with our assumptions, we are thrown for a loop. The disappointment may be so keen that we want to give up.

Satan and his forces are constantly at work to detract us from doing what is right. Sometimes his efforts are as obvious as the strong black horse that challenged Tootle to a race—what we would label as out-and-out evil. But other times Satan's efforts aren't as discernible. Our "good" activities (the buttercups and daisies of our lives) can have distractions lurking in them. Although Satan's work is more subtle and deceptive here, he can distract us just the same.

We can easily recognize Satan's work when we read about how he confronted Jesus in the wilderness (chap. 3). His efforts were obvious as he tempted Jesus to give people bread to get them to follow Him. At the time, Jesus rejected that way of power. Later, however, the temptation came back, and this time Satan's efforts weren't as obvious. Jesus wasn't alone in the wilderness. He was busy doing good and having a successful ministry of teaching and healing.

The relentless crowd

After Jesus chose the 12 apostles, He began training them. He sent them out two by two to minister on their own. When they returned, they were ready to talk. They wanted to share their experiences with Jesus. People, though, clamored around them. "There were so many people coming and going that Jesus and his disciples didn't even have time to eat" (Mark 6:31). Jesus said, "Let us go off by ourselves to some place where we will be alone and you can rest a while." They got into a boat and headed "to a lonely place" (v. 32).

Seeing the boat set sail, the people easily deduced where it was going. Jesus and His disciples were going to the other side of the lake! The people started walking around the lake. It was four miles across the lake by boat. It was ten miles round the top of the lake on foot; however, on a wind-less day, or with a contrary wind, a boat might take some time to make the trip. Energetic people could walk around the top of the lake and be there before the boat arrived, and that's exactly what this crowd did. When Jesus and His men stepped out of the boat, the very crowd from whom they had sought relief was waiting for them.

The crowd pursued Jesus "because they saw his miracles which he did on them that were diseased" (John 6:2 KJV). Their intent was to get something from Him. They wanted Him to heal their sick; they wanted to see His dazzling miracles.

Instead of being annoyed, Jesus' heart was filled with compassion for them (Matthew 14:14). He saw them as "sheep not having a shepherd," and He began to teach them (Mark 6:34) and to heal their sick (Matthew 14:14).

"The day began to wear away" (Luke 9:12 KJV). The crowd of more than 5,000 people became hungry, and Jesus miraculously provided food for them with five loaves and two fish. This miracle triggered tremendous excitement. While they had witnessed Jesus doing unusual things, they hadn't seen anything like this so far! The people concluded, "Surely this is the Prophet who was to come to the world! (John 6:14).

The Jews were waiting for the prophet who would be like Moses. Moses had said, "The Lord thy God will raise up unto thee a Prophet from the midst of thee, of thy brethren, like unto me; unto him ye shall hearken" (Deuteronomy 18:15 KJV). Through Moses, God had miraculously provided bread from heaven (manna). Now, here was Jesus miraculously providing bread.

The people wanted a leader like Moses—someone to give them free food and political deliverance. They longed for a leader who would drive the Romans from Palestine. They wanted someone who would change their status from that of a subject nation to that of a world power. They had seen what Jesus could do, and the thought in their minds was, "If Jesus were our King, with His power, He could make our dreams come true." They were so certain He would make a terrific king, they were ready to make Him king by force (see John 6:15).

The kingdom without the Cross

Because Jesus was the Son of God and because He was sinless, it would be easy to conclude that Jesus' staying on the path God had chosen for Him was a simple matter, but it wasn't. Being sinless meant that He was able to resist temptation (see Hebrews 4:15); it didn't mean He was never truly tempted or that He didn't wrestle with it. Never at any time could Jesus have said to Satan, "You know that I can't sin!"

In this instance, His very nature intensified the struggle. With His compassionate heart, He sensed the crowd's strong desire for a Moses-King, a Bread Messiah. He knew they needed a leader because they were "like sheep without a shepherd" (Mark 6:34). The force of their desire pulled at His heartstrings.

- Wouldn't meeting their need for a leader be as compassionate as feeding their physical hunger?
- Couldn't He do a lot of good for the people, even for God, by becoming a political Messiah?
- What's wrong with using miraculous power to deliver people from the dominion of the Romans? They are God's people; they deserve to be free.
- What's wrong with reducing hunger and curing ills? God does not want people to be hungry or to suffer unnecessarily.

If Jesus were a political king, He could meet the basic needs of the people by political action. He could rid the world of hunger, war, injustice, and poverty without great suffering on His part. Subtly and deceptively through needy people, Satan was trying to detract Jesus from the path of suffering and the Cross. How did Jesus keep from getting off course?

Deliberate, prayerful action

First, Jesus made the disciples get into a boat and go on ahead to the other side of the lake (Matthew 14:22). The fever of a crowd is contagious. Jesus did not want the disciples infected with the Make Jesus King campaign. That would have added to the crowd's momentum and to the pressure on Him.

Next, He calmed the crowd, told them good-bye, and sent them away (Matthew 14:23). Then He went up into the mountain to pray. Here He could be away from the clamor, the constant movement, the chatter, and the needs of the crowd. In this place, Jesus communed with God about Satan's trying to distract Him through needy people.

This struggle was so intense that Jesus spent most of the night in prayer. He might have spent more time if the apostles hadn't needed Him. The apostles had set out back across the lake. While they were rowing, a sudden storm came up. Struggling against the winds and the waves, they made little progress. Seeing the boat fighting the waves, Jesus left the mountain to help.

How long had Jesus intended to pray? Had He planned on spending the whole night? We don't know, but we do know the time spent was long enough to align His will with God's will. He returned to the crowd the next day with renewed determination and strength to stay on course, being the kind of Messiah God wanted Him to be. This is obvious in the courageous and direct way Jesus related to the crowd after His time of prayer.

When they caught up with Jesus in Capernaum (John 6:24), He said,

> *I tell you the truth: you are looking for me because you ate the bread and had all you wanted, not because you understood my works of power. Do not work for food that spoils; instead, work for the food that lasts for eternal life. This food the Son of Man will give you, because God, the Father, has put his mark of approval on him.(vv. 26–27)*

Revealing Himself as the Bread of life was a real crowd separator. The people didn't like the idea of spiritual bread. Many decided Jesus' teaching was just too hard (v. 60a), and others refused to follow Him any longer (v. 66). Nevertheless, Jesus stayed on track. Praying enabled Him to resist Satan's temptation.

The way Jesus responded to the crowd's wanting to make Him king shouldn't surprise us. We've already seen how He frequently withdrew for prayer. It is the most obvious pattern in His prayer life.

The pattern itself has power. When this temptation came to Jesus, He did not have to stop and ask, How should I handle this? "As his custom was," in Luke 4:16 (KJV), may mean not only that Jesus regularly attended Sabbath worship but also that He prayed regularly. As a devout member of the Jewish community, it is likely that Jesus faithfully observed their custom of praying three times a day. These established times of prayer provided Him a disciplined prayer life. The pattern of praying was so ingrained in Jesus that His natural response to distractions was to withdraw for prayer.

Without a pattern of withdrawals in our life, we might be tempted to yield to distractions when they occur. Distractions, by their very nature, discourage us from praying. But if we are in the habit of praying we will pray even when we don't feel like it. We will communicate with God even when we are disappointed and confused. We will stay faithful regardless of the circumstances.

The power of habit

My husband was unhappy in his job at a community college in a large city. Bob wanted to look for another job, but I didn't want to move. We lived near a large theological library where

I had access to thousands of books. The view from my desk was a tree-filled ravine with all its natural beauties. I drew inspiration from the trees and wildlife. I thought I had a perfect situation as a writer.

Bob persisted. After much discussion, we agreed to pray, "Father, if it is your will for Bob to get another job, we pray that you will open the door. We'll not contact any employment agencies. If a new job comes along, it will be totally your doing."

After several months of praying this way, Bob received a phone call from a major Christian university in another state. The school had an administrative opening. To Bob and me that call might as well have been from God Himself! After several interviews Bob was offered the job, and we moved.

The move was difficult for me, and so was the subsequent adjustment. Through it all, I at least had the comfort of believing that we were doing God's will. We had prayed, and God had opened the door. We trusted Him. In time, I told myself, I would adjust.

Bob had been on his new job about six months when he said to me, "I made a mistake in taking this job."

I wanted to say, "You what? How could you have made a mistake when we prayed about this? How could you have made a mistake when God opened this door? Mistakes aren't made when you pray as fervently as we did."

But I didn't say those words. Instead I listened to Bob tell what he suspected. "Something's wrong at work. I can tell my boss is not pleased. I don't know what I'm doing wrong."

I looked out the window at my small, barren backyard that wouldn't even grow grass and grieved for what I had left behind. I thought, *Why did I ever agree to pray with Bob? If I could just go back and do it over, I would be cantankerous and disagreeable. I would insist that we stay where we were.*

Here I was in a place I didn't want to be because we had prayed. The last thing I wanted to do was to continue to pray.

The next morning, though, by habit, doing what I did every day, I met God at my desk for a time of Bible reading, reflection, and prayer. I can't say all my grief and disappointment was resolved in those moments, but it did keep the lines of communication open. It kept me talking with God even when I didn't want to talk.

It was a good thing, too, because Bob was right in what he suspected. His boss told him, "You need to start looking for another job. Your contract will not be renewed."

Look for another job? Possibly another move! I didn't even want to think about it. I was still limp from the last move. I wasn't ready to support Bob through a job hunt or to trust God for a resolution to our dilemma.

Again the force of habit came to my rescue. Day after day, because it was my appointed time, I met God in the early morning and communed with Him. During that time He never gave me a reason for what was happening, but He did help me. I was able to support Bob, continue my writing, care for our children, and teach Sunday School. Time alone with God gave me the strength and determination I needed to continue to be faithful even when I didn't understand what was happening.

This is what the habit of praying will do. It will assist us in keeping on track, but even if a person hasn't developed the habit, all is not lost. What we can't change—what we're dealing with right now—may be God's call to us to begin praying. Now is the time to start. It may be a bit awkward at first because we are not on intimate terms with God. Nevertheless, He will help us. God is always ready to respond to His children. He wants to help us stay on the rails no matter what.

From inspiration to application

What is there about what I can't change that tempts me to get off track?

What might there be about my lifestyle that tempts me to not pray?

How can a habitual devotional life assist me in being faithful even when I want to quit?

What steps can I take to develop the discipline of meeting God on a regular basis?

"O may I ever faithful be,
My Saviour and my God!" [2]

Chapter 8

When God Answers the Person

"God always answers true prayer ... either he changes the circumstances or supplies sufficient power to overcome them; he answers either the petition or the man."[1]

Harry Emerson Fosdick

The spring and summer before John went to college, he experienced a spiritual growth spurt. He earnestly and conscientiously sought God's will. As he led his church's youth group, the older members marveled at his maturity. He seemed so strong and sure of himself.

John took his Christian zeal with him to a large state university. Noticing the extensive immorality on campus, John organized a Bible study in his dorm. He was surprised by how much preparation was required, and college itself was far more demanding than he had thought it would be. Neither had he counted on spending so much time in the lab. After three months, his Bible study dwindled to two others and himself. John felt like he was "running on empty."

Home on break, He described his situation to his senior high Sunday School teacher. He said, "I wish I had someone to tell me if I am doing right. Is this how I should live as a Christian college student?"

As the teacher, Rachel, listened to John, she thought, *I'm 15 years older than he is and I'm wishing for the same thing.* These kids come and go in my Sunday School class. I keep pressing for commitment, but their attitude is "whatever." I get so exasperated. I wish I could change their nature, but I've learned I can't. I have no idea if I am making any kind of impact for Christ on their lives. After they graduate, except for a few like John, I never hear from them again.

Both Rachel and John were unsure of their ministries. They needed reassurance. An inferred prayer of Jesus' indicates that He, too, may have needed some reassurance. It occurred when Jesus was well into the last year of His ministry.

Is anyone catching on?

Many followers drifted away when they saw that Jesus was not leading them toward a Jewish superstate. Those who traveled with Him hadn't caught on to who He really was after nearly three years under His teaching. The opposition of the Jewish leaders had greatly increased in intensity. Jesus was surrounded by an atmosphere of hatred. The powerful Pharisees and Sadducees wanted to get rid of Him. The certainty of the Cross lay ahead.

With time so short, Jesus must have wondered, Does anyone understand Me? Has anyone recognized Me for who and what I am? This was a crucial concern. In *The Mind of Jesus*, William Barclay said,

> *His Kingdom was a kingdom within the hearts of*

men, and, if there was no one who had enthroned him within his heart, then his Kingdom would have ended before it ever began. But if there was someone who had recognized him and who understood him, even if as yet inadequately, then his work was safe. [2]

With His authority, Jesus could have demanded recognition from His followers. He could have repeated who He was over and over until the disciples could spit out the right answer, but that would not have reassured Him. Anyone can memorize facts. Jesus needed God's reassurance that He was accomplishing His mission, so He prayed, and He was not alone when He did.

Alone, but not alone

Jesus withdrew from the crowds to pray, but this time He departed from His usual practice of solitude. He took His disciples with Him. He took them north of Galilee to Caesarea Philippi where He could be alone with them. The Bible says, "As he was alone praying, his disciples were with him" (Luke 9:18 KJV). Why were disciples with Him? And how could He be "alone praying" and yet have them there?

Perhaps Jesus took them with Him because He wanted to set an example. He might have wanted them to connect His strength and His determination to His praying. It would be sometime after this when they would ask, "Lord, teach us to pray" (11:1 KJV).

Perhaps Jesus wanted the disciples there as a buffer. Their presence might have served as protection from the forces opposed to Him or from the constant demands of the people. We've already seen how the crowd doggedly pursued Him when He sought solitude. He might have asked the disciples to be with Him at Caesarea Philippi so He could pray without interruptions.

There's also the possibility that Jesus wanted the comfort of their companionship. One of the reasons He chose them was "that they might be with him" (Mark 3:14 NIV). While solitude is preferable for most of our praying about what we can't change, there will be times when we want the presence of others. They don't even have to be engaged with us in prayer. We just want them there. That's how you can be alone praying and still have people around. Their nearness is comforting and supportive.

Or, perhaps the disciples were present because it was to them He was looking for the reassurance He needed. After all, these were the ones who had been with Him day in and out. They had heard His bold startling teaching, watched Him heal, and watched Him make decisions. The questions on Jesus' mind were, *Are they getting it? Are they catching on to who I am?*

Leading questions

After Jesus prayed, He began asking the disciples questions. First, He asked, "Who do the crowds say I am?" Having mixed with the multitude, the disciples were aware of the various opinions about Jesus. Several answers were given.

"John the Baptist." Here the disciples were probably quoting the ruler Herod Antipas's terrified opinion. He was scared that Jesus was a ghost sent to haunt him for murdering John the Baptist.

"Elijah." Elijah had been taken up without dying, and Malachi said Elijah would return again.

"Jeremiah." Before the Messiah came, some Jews thought Jeremiah would return and reveal where the ark of the covenant and the altar of incense from Solomon's temple were.

"One of the prophets." This was a compliment. If the people regarded Jesus as a prophet, they regarded Him as a man within the confidence of God.

All the answers were intended to be compliments, but that was not what Jesus wanted or needed. Jesus pressed for a deeper answer. To those who had been with Him day by day, He asked, "What about you? Who do you say I am?"

Simon Peter answered, "You are the Christ, the Son of the living God" (Matthew 16:16 NIV).

Peter recognized who He was! Peter was getting it. Here was his reassurance! Jesus exulted in Peter's answer—the Christ, the Messiah, the Anointed One. Jesus said, "Blessed art thou, Simon Barjona: for flesh and blood hath not revealed it unto thee, but *my Father* which is in heaven" (Matthew 16:17 KJV; author's italics). God had answered Jesus.

Jesus had taken His disciples apart for the all-important purpose of finding out if there was any who recognized Him. To His delight, one man did, and Jesus committed His work into the hands of that man.

In His exultation, Jesus made promises to Peter:

- I will build my church on you (Matthew 16:18).
- I will give you the keys of the kingdom of heaven (v. 19).
- Whatever you bind on earth shall be bound in heaven, and whatever you loose on earth shall be loosed in heaven (v. 19).

Interestingly, as joyful as Jesus was, He asked the disciples, including Peter, not to tell anyone that He was the Christ (Matthew 16:20). It was not an announcement; it was not an announcement to be shared with the world at this time.

The sufficient answer

Jesus was joyful that Peter recognized Him as the Christ, the Messiah, even though Peter and the other disciples did not fully comprehend what it meant. When Jesus tried to explain that it involved suffering and death, Peter reproved Him. "Peter took him aside and began to rebuke him. 'God forbid it, Lord!' he said. 'That must never happen to you!'" (Matthew 16:22).

To the disciples Jesus' statements about suffering and death were both incredible and incomprehensible. All their lives they had thought of the Messiah in terms of irresistible conquest, and now Jesus presented ideas that staggered them. Advanced as Peter's insight was, Jesus still had work to do.

God's answer, though, was sufficient. Jesus was reassured. His close followers were beginning to perceive who He really was; He had ignited a torch in their hearts that would never go out. While the flame might have been very small at this time, it was strong enough to serve as a springboard for Jesus to teach His disciples the truth about the future.

"Everyone who asks will receive" (Luke 11:10).

We can learn some helpful things from Jesus' prayer for reassurance and the answer He received. If we take these lessons to heart, a lot of frustration regarding our praying about what we can't change and the answers we receive will be eliminated.

We do not always have to be alone to pray earnestly. Jesus' retreating for prayer with His disciples does not negate the emphasis we've given to praying in lonely places. The dominant pattern of Jesus' prayer life is His praying alone; however, what we are beginning to see—and will continue to see—is some variety in His prayer experiences.

This should be an encouragement to us: we don't have to pray the same way or in the same place every time we pray. There are times when we may want someone with us when we pray.

Those people we mentioned in chapter 5 who are uncomfortable with solitude may find having a friend nearby helpful. While learning to be comfortable alone is a worthy goal, the urgency of the need at hand may call for someone to be near by. His or her presence staves off fear and offers valuable support.

Some of us may need a buffer to keep other people away long enough to carry on a vital conversation with God. A mother of several children, for example, might want her husband or a friend to stand by to handle interruptions so she can have a chunk of time for uninterrupted prayer.

Some people who struggle with an unchangeable that came with a whammy—it was harsh, unpredictable, and sudden—may want a person nearby because they feel fragile. They don't feel strong enough to be alone; they want the assistance of a stronger person standing by.

Other people may need a witness. They know it is time to finally talk with God, to get on with dealing with what they can't change. They said they were going to, but yet have held back. Finally, they proclaim, "This is it. I'm going to turn my burden over to Him. I need you here, to witness this. I'm not even sure I can explain why; it's just I need someone in the flesh to hear my confession as well as God."

God doesn't always answer directly. God answers us in a variety of ways. Often it is that "Abba, Father" type of assurance—the assurance given to us when we've cried out to God for assistance. "God's Spirit" who "joins himself to our spirits to declare that we are God's children" (Romans 8:16) provides us with an inner witness that tells us God has answered. Other times God answers by giving us tools to find what we are seeking. When Jesus prayed for reassurance, God responded by giving Him a tool—questions to ask. When Jesus used those questions, God gave Him the answer He needed.

When John returned to campus, he continued to be haunted by his need to know if he was correctly living the Christian life. Urgently and passionately, he prayed about it. The next morning on the way to the cafeteria, the thought came to John that he ought to talk with Dr. Miller, his major professor and one of the few Christian faculty members on campus.

When John told Dr. Miller about his concern, Dr. Miller responded, "John, I've noticed your struggle to try to keep up with your studies, your lab hours, and also prepare for the Bible studies. You are trying to do too much. I advise you to concentrate on your studies so that you can be a well-trained person to lead Bible studies after college. This doesn't mean you should let up in your moral stand or in your devotional life, but do give up the Bible study. You are not a strong enough student to handle it all."

With a clarity that John hadn't had before, he saw his personal limitations and accepted them. A peace welled up in his heart as he recognized God's answer in Dr. Miller's words. He now knew what to do.

God's answer may not be perfect in the sense that we will no longer have any struggle with what we can't change. When Jesus chose the Twelve (see chap. 6), God's answer was not struggle-free. One of them eventually denied Jesus, and another one betrayed Him to His enemies. When He needed reassurance, it was given through Peter, but Jesus still had to educate the apostles about who He was. It wasn't until the Resurrection that the disciples finally understood what being the Messiah really meant.

Our struggle with unchangeables may not be eliminated by one swooping answer to prayer. God will answer our prayer, but His answer doesn't necessarily mean end of struggle.

Rachel wanted the struggle to end. She longed for the day when there would be no struggle in working with high school students. She kept thinking that if she became good enough as a Sunday School teacher, the struggle would cease. Her class would be perfect, and she would see marvelous results.

Isn't that what many of us want? We want to finally graduate from the school of hard knocks to a postgraduate plain, free from the stress of relationships and challenging growth. Unconsciously, we sometimes pray with this perfect picture in mind.

God's answers, though, may not be perfect in the sense that struggle is eliminated. His answers may be part of a process for some purpose He wants to achieve in our life. Jesus was being made fully adequate for His destined work (Hebrews 2:10). He was learning obedience by the things He suffered (5:8). He was tempted like we are (4:15) and was made like His brothers and sisters so He might be a merciful and faithful High Priest (2:17).

Because we know the outcome in Jesus' life, it would be easy to lose sight of the fact that a process was involved. It's also easy to lose sight of the same possibility in our own life. We may want the perfect answer so much that we fail to see that God might be molding and shaping us into some person we never dreamed about being, or achieving some purpose we never considered.

God's answers will be sufficient. God didn't always answer Jesus directly, nor did He always give Him perfect answers, but He gave Him sufficient answers. The men Jesus chose to be His apostles changed the world. Peter's answer gave Jesus the reassurance He needed.

In both instances—and in instances to come—God gave Jesus what He needed to carry on, even though He did not take away the Cross or its accompanying struggles. God's answers were sufficient to meet Jesus' needs.

That God's answer will be sufficient is a great consolation. His answer may not be specifically what we have asked for, but it will meet our needs.

This truth explains an amazing statement that Adoniram Judson made at the close of his life. This renowned American missionary of the early 1800s said,

> *I never prayed sincerely and earnestly for anything, but it came; at some time—no matter at how distant a day—somehow, in some shape—probably the last I should have devised—it came.* [3]

Judson, though, had prayed for entrance into India and had to go to Burma instead; he had prayed for his wife's life, yet she died and both of their children; he had prayed to be released from the King of Ava's prison. Instead of release, he had laid there months, chained and miserable.

> *Scores of Judson's petitions had gone without an affirmative answer. But Judson always had been answered. He had been upheld, guided, reinforced; unforeseen doors had opened through the very trials he sought to avoid; and the deep desires of his life were being accomplished not in his way but beyond his way.* [4]

As we have seen and will continue to see, Jesus brought His needs regarding His destiny to God through prayer.

God's answers did not always mean the end of struggle. But they were sufficient. God always answered Jesus, and that's what we can count on. God will always answer us.

From inspiration to application

When might I want others with me as I pray? Who would I want to be present?

What mental image do I have of the answer I want from God? Is my image keeping me from seeing God's answer?

What is the difference between a sufficient answer and a perfect answer? Am I willing to trust God for the sufficient answer?

Beyond meeting my immediate need with His answer, what greater purpose may God have in mind for my circumstances?

*"I pray that the God of peace
will give me every good thing I need
so that I can do what he wants. . . .
I pray that God, through Christ,
will do in [me] what pleases him."* [5]

Chapter 9

Needed: A Glimpse of Glory

"When your burden becomes too heavy, when life's ways become too dark, when the heart is too sore, when you are ready to perish, it is not amiss to pray to God to open the heavens, and through a rift in the sky to shine down into your heart some of the light of the Glory World."[1]

B. H. Carroll

Peter's declaration that Jesus was the Christ, the Messiah, must have been some kind of signal for Jesus—a signal to be even more earnest in teaching the disciples. From that time on Jesus began to earnestly explain to His disciples what was ahead.

- "I must go to Jerusalem" (see Matthew 16:21).
- "I must suffer many things at the hands of the elders, chief priests, and scribes" (see Matthew 16:21; Mark 8:31; and Luke 9:22).
- "I will be killed" (see Matthew 16:21).

Jesus attempted to relieve the dark message of death by the bright hope of the resurrection. He said, "But three days later I will be raised to life" (Matthew 16:32). His disciples were too shocked by Jesus' words about suffering and death to hear the words of hope. A suffering Messiah was entirely foreign to their way of thinking. He was to be a conqueror, not one to die at the hands of His enemies.

Surely they thought, *He has taken too gloomy a view of the united opposition of the Pharisees and Sadducees.* Bold, impetuous Peter, as we've already seen, took Jesus aside. He spoke what they all must have been thinking. He said, "God forbid it, Lord! . . . That must never happen to you!" (v. 22).

He "turned around and said to Peter, 'Get away from me, Satan! You are an obstacle in my way, because these thoughts of yours don't come from God, but from man'" (v. 23). Why did Jesus strongly react to Peter's rebuke?

Strong words for strong words

Why did Jesus issue this stinging rebuke, going so far as calling Peter "Satan"? How could Peter have been an obstacle in Jesus' way?

- Perhaps Jesus was grieved that Peter—the one who had made such a noble confession of faith—didn't have a fuller grasp of what being the Messiah meant. Many teachers have moments of discouragement when they wonder, Aren't my students ever going to catch on? All through Jesus' ministry there had been half-veiled intimations about the necessity of His dying (John 3:14; 6:51; Matthew 9:15; John 2:19, Matthew 16:4), but none of these references had been fully understood by the 12 apostles.

- Since Jesus called Peter "Satan," He may have seen Peter's concern as tempting Him to get off course the way Satan had tried to tempt Him in the wilderness. This time, though, the temptation came from one Jesus loved and praised. That made it harder to resist, which may be why He responded so swiftly and decisively.

- When Jesus spoke the words out loud about His suffering and death, perhaps He was reminded of the reality of what was ahead. To be human is to struggle with death. By His strong answer, perhaps Jesus was saying, "This is awful enough as it is, Peter. Don't tempt Me by suggesting there is a way out."

Jesus didn't try to soften His retort; instead, He proceeded to teach what following Him meant:

- Deny yourself (Matthew 16:24).
- Take up your cross (v. 24).
- Lose your life to save it (v. 25).
- Forfeit the world's gain (v. 26).

You can almost hear His listeners gasp, "This teaching is too hard!" This is not what they had expected when they left everything to follow Jesus. Bear a cross? Lose your life? Give up gain? This was asking too much, and it didn't make sense. Where was the reward in following?

Clearly, Jesus had His work cut out for Him. Trying to teach the disciples what the Messiah was like and what true followship meant must have been discouraging for Jesus. About a week after He began His hard, clear teaching, Jesus withdrew to a mountain. It was time for some intense praying, and He took Peter, John, and James with Him.

On the mountaintop

Why did Jesus take these three with Him to the mountain, particularly Peter? I think I would have been tempted to leave Peter behind!

It could have been the protection factor mentioned in chapter 8. They formed a buffer, protecting Him against interruptions.

It could have been the comfort factor. At this time of discouragement, Jesus needed the presence of those committed to working and traveling with Him.

It could have been that Jesus' taking them to the mountaintop reflected His desire to meet their needs as well as His own. If they were recoiling against what He told them, then perhaps prayer would encourage them too.

Certainly Jesus could have prayed for them without their being present, but sometimes the ministry of prayer can be more powerful when we pray for others in their presence.

No matter what Jesus' motive was for taking Peter, John, and James with Him, I don't think the three were looking for much to happen. Weary after the day's activities and the ascent of the mountain, they soon fell asleep. While they slept, Jesus prayed, and God answered in an amazing way.

Jesus' countenance was altered (Luke 9:29). His garments "became shining, exceeding white as snow" (Mark 9:3 KJV) and "dazzling" (Luke 9:29 TLB). Roused by the splendor, the disciples woke up and saw His glory. They also saw Moses and Elijah talking with Jesus. This sparked a conversation between Peter and Jesus. While they were talking, a cloud appeared and covered them with its shadow.

God's voice from the cloud said, "This is my Son, whom I have chosen; listen to him" (v. 35 NIV). Jesus was being encouraged, and so were Peter, James and John. It was a spiritually transforming event.

Jesus' transfiguration

The event gives us a graphic picture of how God encouraged Jesus. Every part of it has meaning.

The change in countenance. As Jesus prayed, an inner change took place. The first outward evidence that God was renewing His strength was a change in His countenance. "His face did shine as the sun" (Matthew 17:2 KJV).

The change in raiment. "There was a kind of effulgence— a celestial radiance—shining out over all. The Divinity within broke through the veil of the flesh and shone out, until His very raiment kindled to the dazzling brightness of the light."[2]

The appearance of Moses and Elijah. Here were two supreme figures among Jews: Moses was the supreme lawgiver, and Elijah was the supreme prophet. Their appearance encouraged Jesus.

> *It is as if they said to him: "It is you who are right, and it is the popular teachers who are wrong; it is you in whom there is the fulfillment of all that the law says and all that the prophets foretold. The real fulfillment of the past is not in the popular idea of might and power, but in your way of sacrificial love."[3]*

Moses' and Elijah's conversation with Jesus. They spoke about the way Jesus would "fulfill God's purpose by dying in Jerusalem" (Luke 9:31). What two better people to talk to Jesus about dying than Moses and Elijah? They were representative of those who witnessed and suffered for God, and for whom the end was not tragedy but triumph. Their words reassured Jesus that if He went on, there would certainly be a cross, but there would also be glory.

The cloud that appeared. This cloud is thought to be the *shechinah* glory of God. All through the history of Israel there was the idea of the *shechinah*, the glory of God. Again and again this glory appeared to the people in the form of a cloud. Now the glory of God was upon Jesus, assuring Him of God's approval on what He was doing.

God's audible words. In the Greek, God's words go something like this: "This is my Son, the dearly beloved one; be constantly hearing Him." God was confirming the rightness of Jesus' interpretation of Himself and of what it means to follow Him.

For Jesus the transfiguration brought new strength and added patience as He moved on toward the Cross. He now had a foretaste of the glory that He would experience after His death.

Encouragement for the disciples

When Peter, James, and John saw Jesus' shining face and His glistening garments, they were "eyewitnesses of his majesty" (2 Peter 1:16 KJV). No Jew would have seen that luminous cloud without thinking of the glory of God resting upon His people, and in that setting, they heard God speak.

"This is my Son" indicates that the voice was for their benefit as well as Jesus'. In the baptism experience the same phrase from Psalm 2:7 had been used, but then it was directed to Jesus. At the baptism, the voice said to Jesus, "You are my Son"; at the transfiguration it said to the disciples, "This is my Son." No wonder Peter, James and John fell on their faces in awe and were afraid. God was speaking to them! And He was giving them instructions. He said, "Listen to him." In the Greek, the tense of this imperative indicates continuous action—"keep on listening to him."

The chain of events starting with Peter's confession indicates that God's instruction to listen referred to their listening to what Jesus was saying about His death. Peter had confessed faith that Jesus was the Son of God, and now the voice from heaven—right out of the cloud of God's presence—confirmed that confession. God wanted them to keep on listening to what Jesus was teaching about the necessity of His death.

Surely this experience lifted the hearts of the disciples. Here was something that would enable them to see the glory beyond shame and humiliation. They still did not fully understand, but the transfiguration gave them some glimmering hope; the future would not be all grim.

God's encouragement to Jesus, Peter, James, and John in response to Jesus' praying should encourage us to pray when we are discouraged.

Encouragement for us

B. H. Carroll described discouraging times in his book *Messages on Prayer.*

> *There are parts of the path of our earthly pilgrimage full of thorns and leading up steep declivities; parts of the way are overshadowed by clouds reaching down into the very valley of the shadow of death. Sometimes we are called upon to bear things that are almost unbearable, and to do things, in the weakness of the flesh, almost impossible; sometimes we sorely hunger for the viands of the heavenly banquet, and crave with intense longing the joys of everlasting and final deliverance.* [4]

While he was writing about the Christian life in general, I think the words, as old-fashioned as they are (I don't think I've ever used the word *viands*), speak of what some of us experience in coming to grips with what we can't change.

It is not wrong at such times to ask for a glimpse of glory. Though the Holy Spirit is given to us as a pledge of all God will ultimately bestow on us (2 Corinthians 1:22; 5:5; Ephesians 1:13–14), we sometimes need a partial glimpse, some transfiguration experience here on earth, to enable us to carry on.

- When we are bogged down in grief over the death of a loved one, we can pray, "Show me in some way that I will see him again."
- When a child break our hearts, when she's done something that can't be undone, something that mars her future, we can pray, "Help me believe her life can be redeemed."
- When our mirror and our energy remind us that we are getting older, we can pray, "Father, show me I will always have significance in your kingdom."
- When we lie awake at night wistfully contemplating "what might have been," we can ask God for a vision for the future.
- When we grow discouraged living the holy life, when we've witnessed and taught with no visible response, we can plead, "God, if you are real, show me yourself all over again."

One of the psalmists said, "I would have despaired unless I had believed that I would see the goodness of the Lord in the land of the living" (Psalm 27:13 NASB). We who are struggling with things we can't change need to see the Lord in the land of struggle. The struggle can get rough. We might be tempted to give up or to give in—to give up the idea of acceptance or to give in to discouragement and despair. The psalmist's advice was to "wait on the Lord" (Psalm 27:14 KJV). In the Old Testament, this phrase frequently refers to prayer. In other words, pray to the Lord so that your heart will take courage and you will be strengthened, which is what Jesus did when He took Peter, James, and John with Him to a mountaintop to pray. This is when it is time to ask God for a glimpse of glory. Through prayer we can be spiritually transformed to handle what we can't change.

How big of a glimpse?

Our glimpse of glory doesn't have to be spectacular like Jesus' transfiguration; a small glimpse will help. A small rift in the sky to let God's glory shine through may be just enough to keep us from giving up. It was for my friend Jan and her daughter Andrea.

Andrea was almost killed in a terrible accident while serving as an international missionary. Afterwards she had to return to the United States because she suffered from post-traumatic stress syndrome. It was a discouraging time for Andrea and her whole family.

Although the doctor for Andrea's missionary support organization was located about three hours away from Jan's home, Jan said she never minded taking Andrea to the doctor. In addition to being medically well qualified, the doctor was a good counselor. She was always able to get Andrea to talk, something the family couldn't do. She and Andrea always prayed together before the session ended.

When Jan dropped Andrea off, she would watch her walk to the door of the doctor's office. Her shoulders were slumped, she dragged her feet, and her face had a grayish tone.

When Andrea came out of the doctor's office, she was smiling, the gray color was gone, and her steps were certain and deliberate. Jan said, "Seeing the change in Andrea was always worth the time and inconvenience of traveling to the doctor. Once Andrea talked and prayed with the doctor, she was encouraged. Her renewed hope was reflected in her appearance. When she had hope, our whole family was encouraged."

One visit with the doctor was not enough to cure Andrea; the healing process was long. Yet each individual visit was enough to encourage Andrea and her family. Each visit enabled them to carry on.

When the glimpse is spectacular

Occasionally, God's encouragement in response to our praying may be spectacular, at least to us. The nature of the experience may be so unusual or dramatic that we may be tempted to magnify it like Peter did. He wanted to prepare three booths, linger on the mountain, and not come down again (Matthew 17:4; Mark 9:5; Luke 9:33). He wanted to prolong the great moment and not return to the everyday world. Likewise, we may want to focus on God's encouragement so much that we lose sight of why God gave it to us.

Or, the relief we experience—whether the glimpse of glory is small or spectacular—may be misleading. We may assume that our struggle with what we can't change is over when it isn't. Experiencing the glory of God did not prompt Jesus to remain on the mountain. It put Him right back on the path He had been walking—the path toward the Cross.

A glimpse of glory is to be a temporary support. It is to give us strength to keep walking. As the Bible says, "Those who *wait for the Lord* will gain new strength; they will mount up with wings like eagles, they will run and not get tired, they will walk and not become weary" (Isaiah 40:31 NASB; author's italics).

From inspiration to application

What does it mean to be spiritually transfigured?

Is transfiguration something that could happen only to Jesus?

How may I seek a glimpse of glory? When should I seek it?

How may I open myself to a transfiguration experience?

"Dark and cheerless is the morn . . .
Till Thy mercy's beams I see;
Till they inward light impart,
Glad my eyes, and warm my heart." [5]

Chapter 10

For So It Seemed Good

"Praise is the highest form of faith; for when we cannot see the answer and yet praise, we are telling God that we trust Him, love Him, and dare leave the final and ultimate answer to Him."[1]

John P. Newport

F inding another job in higher education was difficult. There were many applicants for what openings were available. By the time my husband's university contract had ended (see chap. 7), he had had only two job interviews. A local Bible training school had an opening, but Bob had put off inquiring because the school was not accredited. With no work and no job in sight, Bob applied. The Bible training school hired him as registrar and teacher—a job he liked very much.

Since Bob wouldn't have worked for an unaccredited school before, since he was happy in his new job, since he could make a significant contribution to God's kingdom at a Bible training school, I concluded that this job was what God had originally intended for Bob. The job with the major university was God's way of getting us to the area where the training school was located.

I was so confident of my interpretation that I suggested to Bob that we needed a better place to raise our sons. At the time we were living in a crowded neighborhood with small fenced backyards, even smaller front yards, and cars lining the street. There was no place for growing boys to explore and to play ball.

We bought a house in the country. With a pond beside it, a big yard, and lots of trees, the house provided an idyllic setting for raising boys. In fact, years later, when our oldest son was in college, he wrote a paper about it and called it "The Dreamstead."

When we had been in our new home one year, I was ready to celebrate. I made a cake and planned to serve it— with one candle in the middle—for dinner. I relaxed with the boys in the afternoon. We were outside playing when Bob arrived home.

As the station wagon pulled up, I noticed the back end was filled with books. Looking closer, I saw they were Bob's books.

"Why are you bringing your books home?"

Bob answered, "I've been fired."

His words were like a powerful explosion that blasted away my inner strength. I leaned against the car for support and asked, "What happened?"

"The boss called me into his office about three o'clock. He told me the school wouldn't need me anymore, to clean out my office, and then he handed me my severance pay. He never gave me a reason."

Our evening meal was quiet. The celebration candle was forgotten. Afterwards, I worked in the yard. I knew Bob needed me, but I wanted to be alone with my thoughts. What would we do? Who would ever hire someone who had been fired two times—and so close together? Would we have to move? Leave our country home? In between the questions, a refrain played itself over and over, I can't go through it again. The anxiousness, the uncertainty, and the stress of the first job loss were still fresh in my memory.

Handling stress

Most people can handle major stresses (like being fired!) if they occur several years apart. (Ten years apart is good!) I wasn't emotionally or spiritually ready to support Bob, although practically we managed. To stretch his severance pay, Bob took a temporary, minimum-wage job at a window factory while he looked for another job in higher education. I started babysitting a neighbor's child after school to add to my writing income.

In the afternoons, when Bob arrived home from the window factory and the older children arrived home from school, I fixed hot tea and snacks. Once the children left the table, Bob and I lingered to sip tea and talk. A lot of our talk centered on trying to figure out why Bob had been fired. When the conversation turned to the future, we grew quiet, and a feeling of hopelessness descended on us.

It's not unusual to feel fragile and hopeless when hit by shocking news. News that jars your life may come via the telephone. You hear it ring, you answer, expecting to hear the voice of a friend or someone wanting something, and you hear words that forever alter your life. Or the news may come by a knock on the door. When you open it, a policeman stands there. He says, "I'm sorry to have to tell you, but there's been an accident, a serious accident. Your daughter (or father or spouse) was injured." The jolting news leaves you feeling weak and highly vulnerable.

Bob and I felt like two toothpicks trying to hold each other up. We needed to lean on the other, but neither of us had much strength to offer back. In the past, I would have tried to encourage Bob. I would have expressed confidence in him, in God, and in the future; but I didn't see much of a future for us.

With little hope, I did what I had already learned to do, and that was to "stay on the rails no matter what." Albeit limply, I stuck to my schedule of early morning devotional time, getting Bob off to work and the older children off to school, caring for our youngest at home, researching and writing during the mornings, and doing housework and errands in the early afternoons. In the routine of staying committed, I discovered a key that reduced my fragility, ignited hope, and changed my perspective.

At it happened, I was researching the prayer life of Jesus—the research that would lead to the publication of my book *When Jesus Prayed*. I examined each prayer and looked for patterns in His prayer life. His pattern of frequent withdrawals was easy to spot. As I looked closer, I spotted a second pattern.

A pattern of thanksgiving

Jesus' prayer life revealed a pattern of thanksgiving. In a variety of situations, He expressed gratitude.

When resources were limited. When the crowd of 5,000 men plus women and children gathered to be near Jesus and to experience His healing power, they stayed until it was time to eat. Jesus wanted to feed them. The disciples wanted to send the people away so they could go to nearby farms and villages to buy food. They insisted they didn't have enough food. "'All we have here are five loaves and two fish,' they replied" (Matthew 14:17). Did Jesus change His desire in light of the limited resources? No, He organized the crowd, took the five loaves and two fish, looked up to heaven, and gave thanks. He then told the disciples to pass the food around; there was more than enough for everyone.

When there didn't seem to be enough. On another occasion (Matthew 15:32–39; Mark 8:1–10), sometime after the feeding of the 5,000, another crowd gathered and stayed with Him for three days. Jesus became concerned about their hunger. Among them they had seven loaves. Jesus took the loaves in His hands and gave thanks to God (Mark 8:6). They also had a few small fish (v. 7), and Jesus gave thanks for those also. More than 4,000 people ate and were filled.

When people were unbelieving. Jesus offered precious miracles to the people living in the towns of Chorazin, Bethsaida, and Capernaum (Matthew 11:20–24), and they completely disregarded them. How did Jesus react to this kind of treatment? He pronounced woes upon them, and then surprisingly, He offered thanks:

> *I thank thee, O Father, Lord of heaven and earth, because thou hast hid these things from the wise and prudent, and hast revealed them unto babes. Even so, Father: for so it seemed good in thy sight. (11:25–26 KJV)*

When the 70 returned. The 70 were followers of Jesus whom He had sent out in twos to go ahead of Him to every place where He Himself was about to go. The 70 found, apparently to their surprise, that people did listen and that healings actually occurred. They said to Jesus, "Lord, even the devils are subject unto us through thy name" (Luke 10:17 KJV). Jesus rejoiced in spirit and offered the same prayer He said for those who disregarded His miracles. He said, "I thank thee, O Father, Lord of heaven and earth, that thou hast hid these things from the wise and prudent, and hast revealed them unto babes: even so, Father; for so it seemed good in thy sight" (v. 21 KJV).

When the disciples were irritated. One day in the midst of a crowd, some little children were clamoring to get closer to Jesus. In the judgment of the disciples, Jesus had more important people to see, so they shooed the children away. When Jesus saw what was happening, He said, "Suffer the little children to come unto me, and forbid them not" (Mark 10:14 KJV). Then Jesus took them in His arms and blessed them (v. 16). As He did this, He was crediting God with creating life and acknowledged Him as the one who can make our lives full and happy.

At the tomb of a friend. When Jesus received word that his friend, Lazarus, was ill, He returned to Bethany from Perea. By the time He arrived, Lazarus was dead. Mourners had gathered. Emotion was running high. Jesus wept with Lazarus's sisters, Mary and Martha. Before saying the word of power that would bring Lazarus out of the grave (before the miracle ever occurred), Jesus lifted up his eyes to heaven and said, "Father, I thank thee that thou hast heard me. And I knew that thou hearest me always" (John 11:41–42 KJV). Clearly, Jesus had already prayed for Lazarus to be raised from the dead. In this prayer at the tomb, in front of the gathered crowd and before the actual evidence of the Resurrection, Jesus thanked God.

When the mood was somber. Shortly before His death, Jesus participated in the traditional Passover meal with His disciples. Together they ate the traditional roasted lamb, unleavened bread, wine, and bitter herbs. When the time came for explaining the symbolism of this ancient feast, Jesus departed from tradition. He took a piece of bread in His hand and said a prayer of thanks. He broke the bread, gave it to the disciples, and told them, " 'This is my body.' Then he took the cup [of wine], gave thanks and offered it to them, saying, 'Drink from it, all of you. This is my blood of the covenant, which is poured out for many for the forgiveness of sins'" (Matthew 26:27 NIV).

When sharing a meal. When two discouraged disciples met the resurrected Jesus on the road to Emmaus, they did not know Him. After chatting with Him for a while, they invited Jesus to share a meal with them (Luke 24:30–31). During the blessing and as the food was passed around the table, the eyes of the two disciples were opened. They recognized Him when He sat down with them, picked up a simple loaf of bread, blessed it, and broke it. Remembering other times of thanksgiving—the breaking of five small loaves, the handling of small children, the passing of a cup of wine— they recognized the stranger in their midst.

Gratitude was an integral part of Jesus' prayer life, whether He was walking in the light or in the shadow. Thanksgiving leaped to His lips, not just in life's shining hours, but also during difficult times. I marveled at His ability to praise God in the dark hours, but I couldn't bring myself to say, "Thank You, Father, that Bob lost his job. Thank You that we are in this dilemma." I wasn't thankful, and I didn't expect ever to be thankful.

A little gratitude goes a long way

I was determined, though, not to recommend spiritual principles to my readers unless I was willing to practice them. I still make this a practice; it is a matter of integrity. After pulling together the instances of Jesus' gratitude, it was time to think about application. I had no problem recommending thanksgiving for the good times, but how could I counsel my readers to practice it when times were bleak if I wasn't willing to do it?

As I polished the developing manuscript, typing and retyping the facts, I was drawn to the phrase, "for so it seemed good in thy sight." It comes from the prayer Jesus prayed on a joyful occasion and during a difficult time. I marveled at His attitude. He had confidence that behind whatever was happening was a gracious and benevolent God. Jesus desired to be obedient to His Father's will even if that involved much disappointment and distress. He related everything back to God.

If Jesus could pray those words when His miracles were rejected, perhaps I could at least try saying them. I printed *for so it seemed good in thy sight* on a 3-by-5 card and placed it at the base of the desk lamp. I repeated the words in my morning prayers. Throughout the morning, I spoke the words out loud when I happened to glance toward the card. I whispered them when I hung clothes on the line and when I walked to the mailbox.

Slowly, praying those words made a difference—not a large difference but a significant difference. They ignited just enough hope to change my perspective. Perhaps in some deep, mysterious way God was accomplishing something in our lives that I couldn't begin to fathom or understand.

When that little bit of hope, my inner strength began to return and my feelings of fragility lessened. I stopped saying, "I can't go through it again."

I was now able to encourage Bob. Our afternoon teatimes became planning sessions as Bob and I stopped talking about the past and dreamed again of possibilities for the future. Gratitude made the difference.

From inspiration to application

If I cannot thank God for what I cannot change, is there one thing within my situation that I can thank Him for?

If I am skeptical about the power of gratitude, am I still willing to begin every one of my prayers in the next two weeks with words of thanks?

If I am at a loss for words, am I willing to pray the words of a biblical pray-er such as the ones below?

- Hagar—"Thou God sees me" (Genesis 16:13 KJV).
- Jeremiah—"Great are your purposes and mighty are your deeds" (Jeremiah 32:19 NIV).
- Habakkuk—"Yet I will rejoice in the Lord" (Habakkuk 3:18 NIV).
- Jesus—"Even so, Father; for so it seemed good in thy sight" (Matthew 11:26 KJV).

How might my view of my situation change if I find something within it to be thankful for?

"Yet I will rejoice . . . Father;
for so it seemed good in thy sight." [2]

Chapter 11

Now My Heart Is Troubled

"I have come to bring fire to the earth, and, oh, that my task was completed!

There is a terrible baptism ahead of me, and how I am pent up until it is accomplished!"[1]

Jesus

Sometimes in a movie, the pace picks up and scenes flash quickly, one after the other, on the screen. This technique may be used to save time; many years of history can be covered quickly. It can also create an emotional climate that will help viewers understand what a character is going to say or do.

We need to use this technique of flashing scenes[2] to understand Jesus when He said, "Now my heart is troubled" (John 12:27). This is not something we would expect a regular and grateful pray-er to say. So, what prompted this statement?

A quick look

Scene: Jesus is standing in front of a tomb. The people gathered around are weeping. In a loud voice, Jesus says, "Lazarus, come forth."

The people cheer with astonishment as Lazarus, with his hands and feet wrapped in grave cloths, walks out of the tomb.

Scene: Pharisees and chief priests address the Sanhedrin, the Jewish court. One Pharisee says, "What shall we do? Look at all the miracles this man Jesus is performing! Why some are saying He even brought a man back to life!" Another Pharisee says, "If we let Him go on this way, everyone will believe in Him, and the Roman authorities will destroy our temple and nation."

A chief priest responds, "We can't let that happen. We have to get rid of Him."

Scene: Jesus and His disciples are walking toward a desert. The gate of Jerusalem is behind them. A disciple says to Jesus, "I don't understand why we are leaving. You had more followers than ever after You brought Lazarus back to life. What You did was awesome."

Scene: The streets of Jerusalem are filled with people mingling and talking. One person asks, "What do you think? Will Jesus come to town for Passover?"

Another answers, "Surely not. He won't show His face around here. He's a wanted man. Remember, if we see Him, we are supposed to report it to the Pharisees and chief priests. They will see that He is arrested."

Another person says, "I believe He has the courage to return to Jerusalem; but if He's smart, He'll stay away."

Scene: A resident of Jerusalem says, "Have you heard? Jesus is in Bethany."

"No, you're kidding!" exclaims another.

"Let's go there. It's an easy walk."

"I'm for it. I want to see Jesus; I've heard so much about Him."

"Lazarus is who I want to see. Imagine coming back to life after four days in a tomb!"

Scene: Many people are exiting Jerusalem. A Pharisee in the group turns to another Pharisee and says, "Let's get the Sanhedrin together. I can see we're going to have to get rid of Lazarus in addition to Jesus. Too many of our followers are interested in Jesus because of the miracle of Lazarus."

Scene: The streets of Jerusalem are lined with people. Jesus rides into Jerusalem on a donkey. The people shout, "Praise God! God bless Him who comes in the name of the Lord!" The people spread their cloaks on the road, and they wave palm branches.

Scene: Gazing over Jerusalem, Jesus weeps, "If you only knew what is needed for peace! I ride into town on a donkey so you can see I am on a peaceful mission. If I had chosen a horse, then I might have been representing myself as the warrior you want. O Jerusalem, will you ever understand?"

Scene: At the Temple in Jerusalem, Jesus heals the blind and lame. Little children sing, "Hosanna to the Son of David." Jewish authorities watch. Their arms are crossed; their faces are scowling; their eyes are livid with anger.

Scene: Jesus knocks over the tables of the money changers and the stalls of those selling sacrificial animals in the Temple. As He drives out the merchants and their customers, He says, "The Scriptures declare, 'My temple will be called a place of prayer,' but you have turned it into a den of thieves!"

Scene: Philip and Andrew tell Jesus, "Some Greeks are in town for the Passover. They want to see you." Jesus answers, "The hour has now come for the Son of man to receive great glory. Unless a grain of wheat falls into the ground and dies, it remains a single grain. But if it dies, it produces much grain."

It was at this point, after the request of the Greeks and Jesus' mentioning the grain of wheat that Jesus admitted to having a troubled soul. Various disturbing threads were intermingling, overlapping, and tightening around Him.

The disturbing strands

By looking at the scenes, we can see how complex the situation was becoming in Jesus' life. There wasn't just one thing causing Jesus' tension. Various threads were involved.

The determined opposition. Wherever He was, whatever He was doing, the Jewish authorities were watching, criticizing, and scheming. They were incessant.

The ever-present crowd. Everywhere Jesus went, people followed. He was a curiosity attraction, a phenomenal miracle worker, a daring temple cleanser. Weren't the people ever going to understand His mission and His nature?

His approaching death. Previously, Jesus had spoken of His "hour" (John 2:4; 7:6; 7:30; 8:20). Each time, He indicated that it had not yet come. He had also said that He would lay down His life (10:11, 15) and that other sheep not belonging to the fold (the Gentiles) would join His flock (v. 16). The request of the Greeks (Gentiles) was a signal that it was time for that to happen. To bring them in required His death (12:24). It was time for Him to be the seed deposited into the ground so a great harvest could result.

It was one thing to talk about death; it was another to be the life that gives itself, to be the seed that dies. The stark reality of His imminent death mingled with the hostility of His enemies, the pressure of the crowds, and the frustration of being misunderstood agitated His soul, and He needed relief.

Finding relief

At that moment, Jesus must have wanted to withdraw from the crowd. He must have longed for the relief and refreshment He had found on other occasions in lonely places. But He was not alone. He was surrounded by people. Not being able to escape, Jesus did the next best thing. He prayed where He was: "Now is my soul troubled; and what shall I say? Father, save me from this hour: but for this cause came I unto this hour. Father, glorify thy name" (John 12:27–28 KJV).

Immediately an answer came. A voice from heaven said, "I have both glorified it, and will glorify it again" (v. 28 KJV). God had been glorified by the work of Jesus in the past, and He would be glorified in the future. The crowd standing around heard the voice, but the people were unable to distinguish what was said. Some said it was thunder, while others said, "An angel spoke to him" (v. 29 KJV).

The voice, Jesus said, was for the people (v. 30). However, as dramatic as a voice from heaven might have been, it made no significant change in the people at the time. They went right on misunderstanding (v. 34). Jesus was the one who was helped by his prayer.

God's voice and His words affirmed God's approval and fortified Him for what was ahead. Jesus triumphantly cried, "Now is the judgment of this world" (v. 31 KJV). Confidently He referred to what was ahead. He told them, "When I am lifted up from the earth, I will draw everyone to me" (v. 32). The relief gained from a short, honest prayer steeled Jesus' determination to continue toward the Cross.

A prescription for troubled hearts

It is not unusual to experience disturbing threads of tension when dealing with what we can't change. We may be so perplexed by God's actions in our lives that we want to pull away from Him. At the same time, we long for the peace that only He can give. We may want our will to be done, and yet, we know our desire ought to be the same as Jesus', to glorify God's name. We may want to withdraw from life, but we can't. There are ever-present jobs, deadlines, children, and relationships to deal with. The stress bears in on us, adding to the weight of our dilemma.

Jesus responded to His inner tension with honest praying. Right in the middle of people who did not fully understand Him and, therefore, were not sympathetic to His needs, Jesus confessed His troubled state, wondered what to say, and still sought God's best.

Some say Jesus' feelings and thoughts were not a part of His prayer. Bible translators and commentators disagree over exactly what was His prayer. Some say all of John 12:27–28, beginning with, "Now is my soul troubled" and ending with "glorify thy name," was His prayer. Others say His prayer was simply, "Father, glorify thy name." You may verify this disagreement by noting where the punctuation marks are in different Bible versions of John 12:27–28.

If all the passage was Jesus' prayer, then Jesus honestly expressed His feelings and thoughts to God. He did not suffer in silence and hold back what He was experiencing as if He had to present some kind of "dressed-up, formal" version of Himself to God.

If Jesus' prayer was simply, "Father, glorify thy name," then He must have felt free to confess to others. He said how He felt and then wondered out loud, "Should I pray for escape or should I go on?" He reminded Himself of what He had known for a long time—that He came into the world for this moment—and then He prayed.

Either way, honesty and prayer are linked. Whether Jesus' confession was wrapped up in His prayer to God or He honestly confessed to others and then prayed, He let us know that it is all right to express our thoughts and feelings. In fact, it may be important to dealing with and accepting some things we can't change.

Honesty with God

Throughout the years of studying and preparing for a career in higher education, my husband had a continuing love for preaching. In fact, Bob had taught preaching at the Bible training center where he had been registrar. As we sipped tea in the afternoons when he came home from the window factory, we talked about his skills, his strengths, and his desire to serve the Lord. We wondered if God was using the job losses to channel his love for preaching into a full-time ministry. We talked with our pastor about it, and he, too, seemed to feel this was the case. He advised Bob to make a public commitment to the ministry before our church, and Bob did as he suggested.

That widened the job possibilities for Bob, but none was forthcoming even though he wrote many letters and made many contacts. Eventually Bob had to quit the window factory job because it only paid minimum wage. He became an executive recruiter to support our family.

Meanwhile, the dream lingered for a job in higher educations, but the months turned into years. As Bob recalls it, "I was getting further and further away from what I felt called to do. It was like I was standing on a train platform. The train was going by, and I could see the caboose."

Then a severe recession hit our area. Companies stopped hiring; executive recruiters were no longer needed. There were no jobs to fill.

Bob said, "Were the promises of God applicable to everyone but me? One of my favorite promises was, 'Trust in the Lord with all thine heart; and lean not unto thine own understanding. In all thy ways acknowledge him, and he shall direct thy paths" (Proverbs 3:5–6 KJV). If God was directing my path—where was it?"

Reading the parable of the talents (Matthew 25:14–30) prompted Bob to be honest about his perplexing situation. This parable implies that we will be held accountable for how we use our gifts and abilities, so Bob prayed, "God, I have done everything I know to get a job in a school or a church. If you cannot perform, intervene, or act on my behalf in some way, then when I stand before you on judgment day, I don't want to hear you say, 'Bob, you were not a good steward of the time and talents I gave you.' When you ask me what I have done with my life, I will not be disrespectful, but I will say, 'You explain it; I can't.' I cannot be held accountable for not being given an opportunity to use my talents."

After Bob honestly prayed, nothing outwardly changed, but inwardly everything did. The inner tension that he had been carrying around with him disappeared. He felt at peace with himself and God. Afterward, he said, "The responsibility for what I did with my life was no longer solely mine. If God had called me—and I believed He had—then He shared in the responsibility of what I did with my life."

Honesty with others

Confession of our tension to others—one person or several—followed by prayer may release our tension and fortify us for what's ahead.

The confession may be brief. A complete case history with numerous details may not be necessary in order to bring some relief. In a Wednesday night prayer meeting, in a Sunday School class, in a Bible study, or among close friends, we might say, "I'm struggling with something I can't change. I'm feeling very tense on the inside, and I can't seem to sort out what I'm feeling. I want to do right, but I'm having trouble knowing what that is. I need you to pray with me." A confession like this acts as a release valve. It lets enough tension escape so we can proceed on with coming to terms with what we can't change.

For some, the confession may need to be longer and more detailed to be beneficial. We may need to "talk it out" with a close friend, our pastor or in some cases, a professional counselor. Through talking about the threads of tension we're experiencing with a trusted person, we receive the ministry of good listening, and are encouraged by their understanding. We feel relieved, and hope flares up within us. Verbalizing diminishes the tension that agitates us, freeing us to pray as we ought, "Father, glorify thy name." God responds, bringing us relief and fortifying us to handle what we cannot change.

A word of caution: The relief that comes through confession of feelings and praying doesn't necessarily mean our struggle is over. It could, but it may be with us the same as it was for Jesus. When He prayed "Father, glorify your name," it was Monday. By Thursday night, when His "hour" was looming very near, He needed to deal with the same feelings again. How will He deal with them then? Will honest praying be a tool He will continue to use as He moves closer to the Cross? Will it be one you will use as you try to accept what you cannot change?

From inspiration to application

What is there about my situation that makes me feel "pent up"?

What are the various threads tightening themselves around me, making me feel tense?

How might honest praying, either alone or with others, help me?

If I were going to hear God's audible voice, what would I most like to hear Him say?

"The troubles of my heart are enlarged:
O bring thou me out of my distresses." [3]

Chapter 12

But I Have Prayed for You

"Christ Jesus, who died ... who was raised to life and is at the right side of God, is pleading with him for us! Who, then, can separate us from the love of Christ? Can trouble do it, or hardship or persecution or hunger or poverty or danger or death? ... No, in all these things we have complete victory through him who loved us!"[1]

Paul, the Apostle

When Greg's (from chap. 1) manager told him he didn't have what it took for a professional baseball career, his first thoughts were, *I'll show him.* One way or the other, I'm going to be a professional baseball player.

His second thoughts were of his family. Greg and Cindy had married while college students, right before their junior year. After graduation and while confident of his future, they started planning a family. Cindy was now six months pregnant. Would the energy and time involved in trying to stay in baseball be fair to her and to their child?

While trying to decide what to do, Greg had moments in which he wished he were free to think only of his own interests. That's a luxury few of us have when we are dealing with something we can't change. Our lives are usually intertwined with the lives of others.

As Jesus steeled Himself for the Cross, He had His disciples to consider. They had left their homes and work to follow Him. They had been through much together. What now? What was ahead for them? How would His dying affect them? His concern was evident the evening before His trials and His crucifixion.

His heartfelt concern

Jesus gathered the disciples in a borrowed room for a final meal together. As they ate the traditional Passover meal, Jesus said there was a traitor in their midst, and then He mentioned a prayer that He had prayed:

> *Simon, Simon! Listen! Satan has received permission to test all of you, to separate the good from the bad, as a farmer separated the wheat from the chaff. But I have prayed for you, Simon, that your faith will not fail. And when you turn back to me, you must strengthen your brothers. (Luke 22:31–32)*

In this way, Jesus was cautioning all the disciples about the hours immediately ahead. They were going to be tested like a farmer separating the grain from the chaff. The future would be turbulent for the disciples and especially for Peter.

We are not to think that Jesus did not pray for all the disciples, but Peter was in special danger and particularly needed Jesus' help. Jesus' prayer was not that Satan should be prohibited from testing Peter, but rather that his faith wouldn't fail.

Peter responded by proclaiming absolute loyalty to Jesus. Peter said he was "ready to go to prison" and "to die" with Jesus (v. 33). Peter may have expected Jesus to have commended him for his loyalty. Instead, Peter heard a sobering prediction. "I tell you, Peter," Jesus said, "the rooster will not crow tonight until you have said three times that you do not know me" (v. 34).

Peter's loyalty to Jesus would lapse temporarily, but Jesus was confident it would return. He said, "When you turn back" not "if you turn back." The conjunction is very important in Jesus' statement: "But I have prayed for you." His prayer would ensure Peter's comeback.

Satan might have been granted power to sift the disciples, but Satan would gain only temporary victory. Peter would deny Jesus, but he would repent and come back a humbler and wiser man because Jesus had prayed.

A heart full of love

Later that same evening, Jesus considered the present and future needs of His disciples. He completed the preparation of those dearest and nearest to Him with a final discourse (John 14–16). Here are some of the things He said.

- "I am going to prepare a place for you" (14:2).
- "I will ask the Father, and he will give you another Helper" (14:16).
- "The Helper, the Holy Spirit … will teach you everything, and make you remember all that I have told you" (14:26).
- "But I chose you from this world, and you do not belong to it; that is why the world hates you" (15:19).

Jesus concluded His discourse with a prayer (John 17)—a prayer of loving concern.

Jesus began His prayer by reviewing His mission (vv. 1–5), but his main thrust was for His disciples (vv. 6–19). Jesus expressed gratitude for them (vv. 6–8), and He expressed concern for what they would be up against in the world. "Holy Father, protect them by the power of your name" (v. 11 NIV). Like His prayer for Peter, He didn't ask God to remove them from the struggle, but He did ask that God "protect them from the evil one" (v. 15 NIV).

Jesus asked that His disciples be set apart for God's purpose. "Sanctify them by the truth; your word is truth" (v. 17 NIV). This would enable them to fulfill the enormous responsibility Jesus was going to give them. Jesus was depending on them to continue His ministry and to tell the story of His sacrificial death.

Confident that God would answer His requests, Jesus saw future believers—that includes us!—who would be won through the message and ministry of the disciples (v. 20). In one comprehensive glance, He saw all those the Father was going to give Him. He prayed for them to be united (v. 21). Unity would be important if believers were to penetrate the world with His message.

Jesus also wanted them "to be with me where I am" (v. 24). Jesus wanted a vital relationship with them. Even though He would no longer be present in the body, He could still be present in their lives. Jesus wanted to have intimate fellowship with them, and He could through His Spirit.

The concern and love continue

When Jesus left earth and ascended to the Father, He did not stop praying. What Jesus did for Peter and for the disciples, He does for us. The risen Christ is at the right hand of God, making intercession for us (Romans 8:34; 1 John 2:1; Hebrews 7:25). Having Jesus as our High Priest in heaven should be of great comfort to us.

With so much emphasis put on techniques, requirements, and faithfulness (the rules of prayer), prayer can become a burden. Elaine, a woman in a Sunday School class I once taught, desperately wanted a child. Married and childless for eight years, she prayed fervently for one. She told me, "I'm afraid if I miss one day of devotions, God will not give me a baby." She needed to know that the responsibility of praying was not all hers. We derive now from the Spirit of Christ (the Holy Spirit) the same great support which, during His earthly life, He gave the disciples. He leads us, He speaks to us, and He prays for us.

Jesus sympathizes with and exercises mercy toward us because He knows what human life is like. Jesus experienced every kind of temptation we experience (Hebrews 4:15). He understands what it means to be subjected to pressures that encourage sinning. Being God's Son may have made His personal victory over sin a foregone conclusion but that does not minimize the reality of His temptations—some of which we've already looked at, and there's more to come. "And now he can help those who are tempted, because he himself was tempted and suffered" (Hebrews 2:18).

Jesus exercises His priestly function without interruption or interference. He is a "priest for ever" (Hebrews 7:17 KJV), and He "continueth ever," having "an unchangeable priesthood" (7:24). Therefore, there is never a time when His prayers on our behalf do not reach our heavenly Father. There is never a single moment when He hangs out a Do Not Disturb sign. He is always "on call."

The more we know about Jesus' role of intercessor and the more we acknowledge it, the greater comfort we will experience. Here are some ways we can increase our consciousness of His praying for us.

- We can memorize and recite Bible verses such as Romans 8:34 and Hebrews 7:25 about Jesus' role as intercessor. This role is one seldom emphasized in Christian teaching and preaching, and so we may need to meditate on these verses, keeping them in the forefront of our minds, as we struggle with what we can't change.

- We can meditate on His intercessory role when we take communion. The night Jesus prayed for Peter and for the disciples is when He instituted the Lord's Supper as a memorial meal.

- We can acknowledge His intercessory role when we pray, actually articulating it. For example, our prayer may sound like this: "Lord Jesus, I know right now as I am praying that you are praying too. I know you understand my plight because you know what it is like to walk this earth. It is a great comfort to me not to be alone as I deal with what I can't change." Sometimes when praying this way, I find it hard to be articulate such as when I'm emotionally upset. At times like this, I simply pray repeatedly, "Jesus, plead my case."

- Some believers feel uncomfortable addressing their prayers to Jesus; some even believe it is wrong.[2] They can still recognize Jesus' role by praying this way, "Heavenly Father, I know that Jesus is there at your right hand. I know you are listening to Him as He interprets my case.

I trust you to answer and to respond to
Him as You did to His prayers for Peter
and the disciples."

While increasing our awareness of His role comforts and reassures us, His intercession is not dependent on our knowledge. His intercession goes on whether or not we're aware of it. His love continues whether we're aware of it or not, and it is His love for us that prevents us from turning Him loose when we're struggling with what we can't change.

Tempted to turn loose

While Bob aggressively pursued his work as an executive recruiter, I "went to work" trying to figure out what had happened. When I added up three years of seminary, four years of graduate work, four different jobs in higher education, a call to the ministry, and an executive recruiter's job, it made no sense. Because it didn't, I concluded that God had no purpose in it. Overgeneralizing, I concluded that God didn't have a purpose for our lives.

Rolling stones don't gather moss, but ruminating thoughts do. Mentally, I reviewed Bob's job history, his calling to the different schools, our thinking they were God's will, and no opening for a ministry position. I chewed over and over comments people made to us, "If you just have faith, Bob will get a job. In fact, God probably has a better job waiting for Bob."

To which I mentally responded, *Faith is what got Bob and me into this dilemma. We prayed and sought God's leadership at every step.* If I said as much, then I was accused of having a "negative spirit" and was directed to get my life straightened out.

While some insisted our problem was a lack of faith, others told us that getting a position depended on "who you know." In our attempt to be conscientious Christians, we had not given thought to making "connections" for our future. We were sincere, hardworking Christians. We did our jobs quietly without fanfare, had a simple lifestyle, and were family oriented. Those qualities, we learned, were not good enough to ensure success.

Overreacting, I became critical of many of the religious leaders who were deemed successful. It did not seem to matter what kind of life some of these leaders lived. The "sheep" seem to make no distinction over what kind of "shepherd" they followed. If the leader's words were spoken with authority, if they were preceded with, "God told me . . ." then they were accepted and followed whether or not the words were in accord with the nature and teachings of Jesus. Power and personality in the leader were the important things. It looked as though what it took to succeed in the Christian realm was the same as what it took to succeed in the secular realm— assertiveness, successful image, political connections, being a good promoter and a people manipulator.

I brooded over how naïve I had been to have believed it could have been otherwise. Being conscientious and having a sincere desire to serve the Lord were not enough to keep a job in a Christian setting or to enter the ministry. With the loss of my naïveté, I became depressed.

During the week, I would make progress fighting my depression. When I went to church on Sundays, I would regress when I heard statements like, "God doesn't sponsor losers." Eventually I began to see that my disturbing thoughts were linked with my Christian activities. If I quit going to church, perhaps I could break free from depression's grip.

In my mind's eye, I pictured the Christian activities I would eliminate from my life—Sunday School, morning and evening worship, Bible studies, etc., then across the picture came Jesus, dusty and bloody, carrying His cross, wearing His crown of thorns, experiencing the ultimate in rejection. With weary, sad eyes, He said to me, "Brenda, I thought we were in this together." With those words and that look, I knew that I could never quit.

I am a Christian today and a faithful church member because Jesus held on to me. His intercessory love was in effect even when I was not aware of it. I'm so glad His life was—and is—still wrapped up in the lives of others.

When we find ourselves in a wilderness overrun with hazards which threaten to overwhelm us, when we are "pent up" with tension, when we can't see light at the end of the tunnel, when we're filled with anger because progress isn't happening fast enough, or when we feel discouraged about ever finding inner peace, this is when we must count on the intercession of our High Priest.

Let us, then, hold firmly to the faith we profess. For we have a great High Priest who has gone into the very presence of God—Jesus, the Son of God . . . Let us . . . approach God's throne, where there is grace. There we will receive mercy and find grace to help us just when we need it. (Hebrews 4:14–16)

From inspiration to application

How does Jesus' intercession for me differ from how others might pray for me?

What difference does the fact that Jesus is praying for me make in my ability to cope?

How may I increase my awareness of Jesus' intercessory role?

"Thou art a priest for ever." [3]
"Ever for us interceding." [4]

Chapter 13

Expressing Emotions: A Necessary Release

"I had been lamenting the wounds of my childhood and parading them before God. As self-pity overthrew me, I wept violent tears held back for 20 years. I accused God of injustice. 'He crushed me,' I shouted aloud, 'and you stood by watching! He rejected me, and you remained silent! . . .' For an hour or more the bitterness flowed, till my eyes were swollen. When I finally collapsed into silence, the Lord answered me."[1]

Paul Thigpen

Jesus was a man of joy, fully experiencing life. He was compassionate and caring. He got angry, visibly so at times, and He also experienced sorrow. Late Thursday night, before His death on Friday, He said to His disciples, "The sorrow in my heart is so great that it almost crushes me" (Mark 14:34). This heavy sorrow was connected to His unchangeable—the Cross, and yet earlier in the week, His tension regarding the Cross had been resolved or so we thought. What happened?

Following Monday

On Monday in Jerusalem, in front of a group of people, Jesus admitted His heart was troubled. When He prayed, the tension was resolved, and He was ready to face what was ahead. The days, though, that followed were stressful, and His soul became troubled once again.

On Tuesday several groups tried to trap Him. They wanted to get Him arrested or have Him discredited in front of the people. That same day He passionately denounced the Scribes and Pharisees, pronouncing woes on them. He spoke to His disciples about His second coming, the forthcoming destruction of Jerusalem, and reminded them of His death.

On Wednesday, in the home of Simon the leper, Mary of Bethany anointed Him for burial. She was aware as He was that death was near.

During the Passover meal early Thursday evening, Jesus identified a traitor in their midst. He said to Judas, "Go and do what you have to do."

Afterwards, Jesus lovingly dealt with needs of the remaining disciples, teaching them, praying for them, and preparing them for the future. All of these activities reminded Jesus, "Your hour is near." Death, an awful death by crucifixion, was staring Him in the face. Consequently, by late Thursday night, deep sorrow and anguish over-took Him. He was even more troubled than He had been on Monday.

Jesus responded to this turmoil the way He responded to other concerns He had faced. He prayed. Looking at this prayer experience, we get a fuller picture of what was troubling His soul and the kind of praying needed to gain relief.

In the garden

Outside the city was a place Jesus had frequented in the past when He needed renewal (Luke 22:39). The place was the Garden of Gethsemane. This garden didn't belong to Him. Well-to-do people had gardens on the slopes of the Mount of Olives, and one of them must have been a friend of Jesus' or a follower who gave Him permission to use it.

Jesus' apostles went with Him. As they entered the garden, Jesus asked the disciples to sit and wait. He said, "Stay here and keep watch" (Mark 14:34). Judas might be returning with the Jewish authorities. He needed some protected time to pray, to be ready, which meant dealing with what troubled Him.

Peter, James, and John went with Him further into the garden. At this time, Jesus became emotional. He was filled with "distress and anguish" (v. 33). "He began to be sorrowful and troubled" (Matthew 26:37 NIV). "Grief and anguish came over him, and he said to them, 'The sorrow in my heart is so great that it almost crushes me" (vv. 37–38).

"He went a little farther on, threw himself on the ground, and prayed" (Mark 14:35). The verb tense Mark used indicates repeated or continuous action. In other words, Jesus was deeply agitated.

Jesus began to pray that it might not have to be the way of the Cross, that He might accomplish God's will some other way. He pleaded for God to take the cup from Him. He prayed this way confident that God could and would respond to Him. If another way were possible, God would grant it. "'Abba, Father,' he said, 'Everything is possible for you. Take this cup from me'" (v. 36 NIV).

The prayer was for a way out. Jesus' prayer was honest and forthright; He wanted to avoid what was ahead. But—

and this is very important—He also wanted to do God's will. This is what made His struggle so complex, so in addition to praying for an escape, He also prayed, "Yet not what I will, but what you will" (Mark 14:36 NIV).

This was no easy praying, although it might appear this way on a first or second reading. Because so few words are printed, we can get the idea that His praying was short and pithy like what He prayed in front of people on Monday. What's printed ("Take this cup from me. Yet not what I will, but what you will") was the essence of what He was praying. The desire to escape and the desire to please God were at odds. If the praying was short, the disciples wouldn't have fallen asleep, and that's just what they did.

He returned to Peter, James, and John, and said, "How is it that you three were not able to keep watch with me for even one hour?" (Matthew 26:40). The disciples didn't understand what Jesus was struggling with, and the struggle wasn't over. Resolution didn't come quickly.

Once more He went away, "and *being in an agony he prayed more earnestly*" (Luke 22:44; author's italics). Jesus progressed in His struggle from the first prayer into an even more intensive combat, so rigorous that "an angel from heaven appeared to him and strengthened him" (v. 43) allowing Him to pray even more intensely.

The degree of intensity was so severe that "his sweat was as . . . great drops of blood falling down to the ground" (v. 44). Under great stress, tiny capillaries in the sweat glands can break, mixing the blood and the sweat. This process alone is enough to produce marked weakness and possible shock, and yet Jesus' need was so great that He continued to pray. He needed a way out or He needed strength to face what He could not change. He needed God to answer Him.

A way out

What was Jesus wanting to avoid? What was the "cup" He asked to be removed?

The "cup" could have been the rejection and public execution Jesus would have to experience. To die on the Cross, He must surrender Himself to dreadful shame, to abuse, and to excruciating pain.

Some commentators say He dreaded the heinousness of becoming the scapegoat, the sacrificial lamb who would bear the sins of the world.

It could also have been a reluctance to die that all mentally healthy people have. The desire to live is built into human nature. No one wishes to die; no one wishes to die at 33 years old. While Jesus had known all along that He must suffer and die, He resisted it as the Cross loomed near.

All three of these explanations could explain why He was filled with such dread. One thing is certain: Escape routes were open to Jesus. If they weren't, that would have made a mockery of His willingly choosing to die for us (John 10:17–18). In the darkness of the night, He could have slipped out of Jerusalem. He could have compromised with the religious leaders and diluted their hostility. He could have called on regiments of angels to come to His defense (Matthew 26:51–54), but He didn't because He wanted to please God.

And yet . . .

In addition to wanting an escape, Jesus also wanted to do what God wanted. He prayed, "Yet not what I want, but what you want" (Matthew 26:39). Jesus knew the Cross was essential to the plan, purpose, and design of God, whom He wanted to please. If He wanted to be the obedient Son, escape was not possible. He could not change His destiny if He wanted to be obedient.

If He knew that death on the Cross was God's will for Him, why couldn't He just go ahead and do it? Why the emotional turmoil? We must keep in mind that Jesus fully entered the human situation, experiencing the emotions we have. He wasn't programmed so He automatically did the right thing as if He could not disobey. Every act of obedience was a response of the will, not a conditioned reflex. Satan knew this, and that's why he pulled out all the stops, tempting Him in the Garden of Gethsemane, as he had on other occasions, in attempt to get Jesus off course. The fact that Jesus was without sin means He knew depths and assaults of temptation that we will never know. We fall to temptation long before Satan has put out the whole of his power. Jesus' battle with temptation wasn't easier because He was sinless; it was immeasurably harder.

In his commentary on Luke, William Barclay says, "There is no scene like this in all history.... [Jesus] could have turned back even yet. He could have refused the Cross. The salvation of the whole world hung in the balance"[2] and Satan knew this. Jesus persevered, though, and resisted temptation by being honest and admitting His struggle to the One who could help Him.

God responded by giving Jesus a way through rather than a way out. After Jesus' plea for escape, God strengthened Him in such a way that Jesus calmly proceeded toward the Cross. As the drama of His last hours unfolded, Jesus, more than the Roman procurator Pilate, more than those who sought His arrest, appeared to be in control. Throughout the entire course of the arrest and trials, Jesus was the picture of a man on top of the situation. The emotional state of Jesus when He entered the garden that night and when He left in chains was entirely different. He entered distressed and anxious—perhaps terrified as some commentators say; He left the garden composed and with quiet confidence. He knew He could accomplish God's will because He prayed and God answered. God wants to do the same for us, and He will if we follow Jesus' example.

Learning from Jesus

From Jesus' Gethsemane experience, we learn that the struggle with what we can't change can become very intense. This is not a given. Not all of us will experience emotional turmoil, but some of us may find ourselves in an agony. We may experience a depth of feeling that we didn't know existed. We may experience sorrow in our hearts so great that it almost crushes us.

Jesus' experience in Gethsemane shows how much emotion is wrapped up with the spiritual. Surrendering to God's will was—and is—basically a spiritual struggle, but emotions are involved. The feelings that accompany unchangeables may be intense; they may be agonizing, but they are normal.

Jesus didn't see His emotions as something to hide. If He did, He would not have taken His disciples with Him to the garden. His emotional struggle takes nothing away from Him as a person. If anything, it enhances Him. It makes me appreciate all the more what it cost Him to die on the Cross.

The twofold nature of Jesus' prayer shows us that He admitted His struggle to God. He felt no need for cover-up or pretense. If Jesus, who knew the Father intimately, offered His prayer in this manner, then we should feel free to do likewise.

If we haven't been able to come to terms with what we can't change, then perhaps it is time we found a place, our own Garden of Gethsemane, where we can pray honestly. We need a place where we can recognize our feelings, sort them out, and release them. We need a place where we can be honest with God.

Being honest with God

Some of us may be hesitant to express our emotions to God, but there is no need to hide them from Him, since He is aware of their existence even before we are (Matthew 6:8). The Bible says that "all things are naked and opened unto the eyes of him with whom we have to do" (Hebrews 4:13), so we do not need to conceal anything from God. With reverence and respect, we may bare our hearts before Him and tell Him how we feel.

Ronald Dunn discovered this valuable and liberating truth in the aftermath of the death of his son. He writes,

> *I learned . . . It's okay to tell God how you feel. After all, He already knows. I've never told God anything He didn't already know. I've never heard God gasp in surprise at anything I said. I've never heard God say in response to any confession, 'I would never have believed that of you.*[3]

Jesus offered up His prayers with "strong crying and tears" (Hebrews 5:7). He released His emotions, something we may be reluctant to do. The emotions that accompany what we can't change may be unpleasant ones, like anger, grief, or fear. Because they feel so terrible, we might be tempted to keep a lid on them rather than let them surface, but they need to be released. Ignoring them can set us up for further difficulties, and their presence can prevent God's help from getting through.

John M. Koessler was the product of a dysfunctional family, something he couldn't change. In a *Decision* magazine article, Koessler described how he hid his emotions rather than releasing them. He stuffed them into a "secret closet hidden in the dark recesses" of his soul. [4] He said, "Eventually the closet became too full to accept another repressed emotion, and my repressed emotions started tumbling out. If I allowed myself the liberty of a little anger, it swelled into a torrent of rage. A moment of sadness spiraled into deep depression." [5]

Failure to release the emotions that accompany what we can't change may set us up for depression, cynicism, deep bitterness, chronic irritability, and even medical problems. Even worse, unreleased emotions can block our channel for receiving God's help.

Opening the channel

Unreleased emotions swell, filling the channel God needs to minister to us. Releasing our emotions opens up the channel so God can respond. As Karen Burton Mains writes,

> *How many times he refused to respond to my prayer requests, often for weeks or months. Then when I finally spilled forth my anguished frustrations, suddenly the heavens opened and he overwhelmed me with his love.* [6]

A crusty magazine reporter discovered this when he was dying from a hepatitis virus that was destroying his liver. As a journalism student, he had been taught to be objective. He had learned not to express emotions. A lay hospital chaplain told him, "Don't be afraid to show your feelings. God gave us tears to wash our pain away."

After the reporter learned to express his emotions in prayer, he said that in a way nothing had changed. He was still going to die. But in another sense, everything changed because he now had hope. He believed he could grow and gain from the experience ahead, and he did. [7]

How honest?

Jesus was so honest in expressing His feelings that He asked for a way out, and in some situations that may help us too. It seems odd to suggest praying for escape from something we can't change, yet it helps. Knowing something is unchangeable causes us to fight against it rather than accept it. This continual resistance creates a pressure buildup and increases the difficulty of adjustment. Praying for an escape releases the pressure. Once the pressure is released, repressed emotions can escape, clearing the channel for God to respond.

When I discussed this concept with a friend, she said, "My prayer journal is filled with escape requests. Some of those pleas were granted, but the majority were not. God, however, always gave me the grace and strength to deal with what I couldn't change. He always answered me." When the pressure was released, when the emotions were honestly expressed, God strengthened her just as He did Jesus and just as He wants to strengthen us.

Jesus' victory at this juncture didn't come quickly nor did it come easily, but it came. Our wrestling may be similar; we may experience several battles before we accept what we cannot change so we shouldn't be surprised when a battle reoccurs. Neither does it mean that we should discount the gain or relief experienced at any one battle. God gives us what we need at each critical juncture. God answers sufficiently. That the battle comes back simply indicates the nature of what we are up against. Some battles are harder to win than others, but victory is still possible. There will come a time when the warring ceases.

Life's hardest task may be to accept what we cannot understand; yet we can if we pray like Jesus did.

> *He went into Gethsemane in the dark; He came out in the light ... He went into Gethsemane in an agony; He came out with the victory won, and with peace in His soul—because He had talked with God.* [8]

I want to walk in the light, don't you? I want to have peace in my soul, but before I came to this conclusion, I had to recognize some emotions that needed to be dealt with. It would take another of Jesus' emotional prayers—one yet to come—for me to recognize this and find peace.

From inspiration to application

What is so awful about what I can't change that makes me want to escape?

What emotions am I experiencing?

Why am I hesitant to express those feelings in prayer?

Why would expressing my feelings in prayer help me?

"Father . . . my Father!
All things are possible for you.
Take this cup of suffering from me!
Yet not what I want,
but what you want." [9]

Chapter 14

Father, Forgive Them

"When you forgive, you reclaim your power to choose. It doesn't matter whether someone deserves forgiveness, you deserve to be free." [1]

Mary Grunte

Jesus had just finished His prayer battle in the Garden of Gethsemane when a large crowd arrived. They were armed with swords and clubs and were intent on finding Him. Judas, one of Jesus' apostles, was their leader. He had arranged a signal with them, "The man I kiss is the one you want" (Matthew 26:48).

When Judas kissed Him, Jesus said, "Is it with a kiss that you betray the Son of Man?" (Luke 22:48).

The chief priests, the elders and the temple police arrested Jesus, and all the disciples left Him and ran away (Matthew 26:55–56).

The crowd whisked Jesus away for some hastily arranged trials before the Sanhedrin, the governing body of the Jews.

Ignoring their own judicial standards, the religious leaders didn't seek any witnesses on Jesus' behalf. They paid false witnesses to testify against Him and found Him guilty on false charges. Then they took Him to the Roman procurator, Pontius Pilate—a step necessary to legally bring about Jesus' death.

Pilate sensed that Jesus was innocent, but not wanting to court disfavor with the Jews, he tried to avoid making a decision. He sent Jesus to Herod Antipas, tetrarch from Galilee, who was in Jerusalem for the Passover. Herod sent Jesus back to Pilate. Roman soldiers tormented Jesus during His appearances before both Pilate and Herod. They stripped Him of His clothes and forced Him to wear a crown of thorns.

Still convinced of Jesus' innocence but wanting to please the Jews, Pilate gave the crowd a choice. "Which one do you want me to set free for you? Barabbas or Jesus called the Christ?" (Matthew 27:17).

"'Barabbas!' they answered" (v. 21).

"'What, then, shall I do with Jesus called the Messiah?' Pilate asked them. 'Crucify him!' they all answered" (v. 22).

Pilate gave in and sentenced Jesus to death (Luke 23:24). Pilate had Jesus whipped and then turned Him over to His executioners. They immediately took Him to the crucifixion site.

Jesus' hands were nailed (and probably tied) securely to the horizontal bar of the Cross. He was hoisted between two thieves. His feet were twisted, with a long spike driven through them into the Cross. In this position, He could barely move.

But He was a miracle worker, wasn't He? Couldn't He do a superman stunt, flex His muscles, and come down from the Cross? That's what the passersby wanted to know.

They "shouted abuse, shaking their heads in mockery. 'Ha! Look at you now!' they yelled at him. 'You can destroy the Temple and rebuild it in three days, can you? Well then, save yourself, and come down from the cross!'" (Mark 15:29–30 NLT).

But Jesus didn't save Himself. His hour had come. He was caught tightly in the vise of what He could not change. In its clutches, how did Jesus respond to betrayal, desertion, unfairness, ridicule, and pain?

He prayed, "Father, forgive them; for they know not what they do" (Luke 23:34 KJV).

It's the same response that some of us may need to make.

Who might need to forgive

Not everyone who struggles with unchangeables will need to forgive, but some will. If your unchangeable involves mistreatment, abuse, injustice, or wrongdoing, then forgiveness may be necessary to find peace as these three examples suggest.

CYNTHIA BARELY LOOKED UP when her husband yelled good-bye on his way out the door. George was running late for a business appointment in the next town, but Cynthia wasn't concerned. It was a clear day, and the roads were dry so George should make good time. Fifty-five minutes later, a policeman appeared at her door. "I'm sorry, ma'am, but your husband has been in a terrible accident on the interstate. He was killed."

Cynthia braced herself against the door frame to keep from falling. "What happened?" she asked.

"We don't know why, but a truck was traveling the wrong way on the interstate. As best as we can determine, your husband didn't see him coming because he was behind several cars. When he pulled out to pass, there was the truck, and the two collided. Your husband died instantly. The truck driver is still alive at this time, but his injuries are very serious."

❧

KARL AND THOMAS AND THEIR WIVES were the kind of friends who often spent evenings talking after a good meal while their children played nearby. Thomas admitted in one of those talk sessions that he was worried about losing his job. He said, "No matter how hard I try. I can't seem to please my boss."

Considering his friend's skills, Karl said, "Don't worry. If it should come to that, I'll find you a place where I work." Thomas relaxed. He knew he could count on his friend.

Six months later when Thomas was fired, Karl said, "What a tough break. I'll be praying for you." Not a word was said about a job.

❧

TRUDY WAS A PRETTY LITTLE GIRL, sweet and cuddly. Everyone wanted to hold her and to play with her when her large, extended family gathered for reunions. Uncle Lawrence, though, was the only one who took her for long walks. He took her to the pasture to see the cows and behind the barn to look at the little piggies. Out of sight from other family members, he fondled her in inappropriate ways. Trudy's innocence was robbed by a man who knew better.

~

INCIDENTS SUCH AS THE THREE ABOVE leave people struggling with unsettling emotions.

Anger. Cynthia was angry. How could a person be so careless to drive the wrong way on an interstate, risking the lives of many and killing George? Now her children were fatherless, and she was left without a husband.

Trudy, too, was angry. Her anger had been simmering for years. How could her uncle have abused her? Why didn't her parents protect her? Why didn't some other relative notice what was happening and rescue her?

Demand for justice. Our hearts cry out for justice when we have been wronged. Uncle Lawrence ought to be punished. The reckless truck driver should have to pay with his life.

Grief. Cynthia's loss was great. She wept for herself, for her children, and for the life they would have had if George had lived.

Thomas grieved over Karl's silence. He thought more about Karl's promise than he did about what he couldn't change—the job he had lost, or what he could change—getting a new job. How could his friend forget so quickly what he had said? How could he ignore his situation?

Initially, these emotions are healthy responses if we release them in appropriate ways. (Honest praying, we've learned in the last chapter, is a healthy release.) But if we don't release these emotions, then we may "grow" another problem: unforgiveness.

Our grief turns into bitterness or cynicism. Our anger intensifies and smolders. Our legitimate desire for justice turns into a desire for revenge. We nurse our hurt by reliving the wrong over and over, robbing us of peace of mind. Unforgiveness distorts our vision, warps our thinking, and pollutes our soul. The pain and the hurt control us.

The obvious remedy for escaping this bondage is forgiveness.

- It breaks the ruminating cycle.
- It frees up energy.
- It restores peace of mind.
- It renews our vision.
- It removes the venom poising our souls.
- It enables us to move forward instead of holding on to the past.

With so many benefits, why might people hesitate to forgive?

We may hesitate because the bondage itself is so strong. Already caught in the vise of what we can't change, unforgiveness tightens its grip. To break that kind of bondage is tough to do.

We may hesitate because forgiveness ignores our hurt. It suggests that anything can happen to us or be done to us, and it is not important.

Another reason we may hesitate to forgive is that we fear the forgiven will not have to be accountable or punished. We equate forgiveness with saying, "Oh, never mind. It's all right. What you did doesn't really matter."

I sympathize with these hesitancies so much that I was reluctant to write this chapter. And yet if we are going to walk with Jesus all the way from His baptism to the Cross, this is a step we must imitate. Unless we forgive, our coping with what we can't change will be incomplete. Peace of mind will elude us and ability to move forward will be limited. We'll also limit the amount of help God can give us.

Imitating Jesus

Jesus' prayer of forgiveness does not tell us everything we need to know about forgiving, but it does give us some important help.

Start where you are and not where you should be. Jesus didn't pray, "Father, help me to forgive those who have brought about my death and mistreated me." Instead, He prayed, "Father, forgive them."

These are good words for us to use in getting started. We do not have to feel like forgiving to initiate the process. We do not have to begin with "I forgive." We can begin with "Father, forgive them." When we take the right actions, the right emotions will follow.

This is not to suggest that Jesus wasn't expressing His forgiveness when He prayed. Earlier in His ministry, He had taught, "Pray for those who abuse you" (see Luke 6:28), and on the Cross, He did exactly that.

His example, though, suggests a tool for us to use. When we don't have the words to say, when we don't have the heart to forgive, praying Jesus' words will get us started.

Acknowledge God's sovereign rule. Jesus prayed for God's forgiveness for His tormentors and executioners because they were going to need it. Jesus knew that those who abused Him and ridiculed Him would be held accountable for their actions. This is verified by early New Testament preachers. They tried to stab men's minds with the realization of the sheer crime of the Cross. Every mention of the crucifixion in Acts is instinctive with horror at the crime committed (compare Acts 2:23; 3:13; 4:10; 5:30).

Praying "Father, forgive them" acknowledges that what people do does matter. In a world where men and women hurl injustices on others, God will hold them accountable and execute punishment (Romans 12:19).

We have laws and legal options that help make people accountable, but those have their limits. Cynthia discovered this when she brought a civil suit against the truck driver who killed her husband. She won a large settlement because of his negligence, but it wasn't enough to eliminate her bitterness. She knew she had to release the driver to God, the one to whom we are all ultimately accountable. She didn't feel like forgiving the truck driver, but she asked God to forgive him. She prayed "Father, forgive him" because it was the right thing to do. It is what Jesus would have done. As she disciplined herself to pray those words day after day, eventually her bitterness melted and she embraced life.

Try to gain insight concerning those who wronged you. In His prayer asking God to forgive those who wronged Him, Jesus included a significant phrase: "For they know not what they do"(Luke 23:34 KJV). Jesus looked upon those who wanted Him to die as victims of a system. They were blinded by the ceremonial restrictions of the law. They were blinded by years of tradition of what they perceived God to be like, blinded by what was really a fabrication. Jesus looked and saw them responding to the circumstances and forces around them. They were unaware of the dreadful consequences of their act. They did not, in their ignorance, know that they were bringing suffering and death to the Son of God.

If we can gain insight concerning those who have wronged us, we gain a valuable tool for forgiving them. What forces shaped their lives? What drove them to do what they did? If we could know all that is in their hearts, if we could walk in their shoes for a while, perhaps seeing some of their pain, we might be more tender in our judgment.

I wonder if this isn't one reason why Jesus suggested confrontation when forgiveness is needed (Matthew 18:15; Luke 17:3). Confrontation leads to communication. In talking with the person who wronged us, we may gain understanding of the forces that shaped and motivated him or her.

In order to forgive Karl, Thomas decided he would have to confront him—let him know how he had hurt him. He asked Karl to meet him for coffee. Thomas said, "I don't understand how you forgot about your offer to get me a job. Did I misunderstand?"

Karl answered, "No, you didn't misunderstand As it turned out, I don't have as much influence at work as I thought I did. In fact, I'm now worried about my own job. Things are shaky and unsettled at the office. Everyone is suspicious of each other. I shouldn't have said what I did to you that night. Afterwards, I was ashamed to admit to you how little influence I have."

Hearing those words, Thomas saw that his friend hadn't deliberately meant to hurt him, and he forgave him. Thomas was able to take the emotional energy he had been using for ruminating and channel it into his search for a new job.

Trudy, though, couldn't confront Uncle Lawrence because he died when she was a teenager. The counselor she was seeing for depression suggested that she find out what she could about Uncle Lawrence's past. After some discreet investigation, Trudy discovered that he had been the victim of sexual abuse and that he had trouble relating to adults. Making this discovery wasn't the only tool Trudy used to forgive him, but it was an important one. It broke that incessant ruminating which contributed to the smoldering fire of unforgiveness. Over and over she had asked, *How could he do such a thing?* Now she knew.

Forgiveness does not suggest that wrongdoers go unpunished, but it does call for understanding of the pressures that lead to the transgression. When the unforgiving spirit is threatening to turn our hearts to bitterness, let us hear again Jesus praying for forgiveness for those who crucified Him, and let us follow His example. When we do, we'll be able to let go of our painful emotions and move on with our lives.

From inspiration to application

When trying to come to terms with what I can't change, do I need to consider forgiveness?

Whom do I need to forgive?

How can Jesus' example help me to forgive when it seems impossible?

What can I pray when I can't say, "I forgive"?

"Lord, do not hold this sin against them." [2]

Chapter 15

Totally Abandoned?

"Every humble man who suffers moments of perplexity and doubt, or even despair, can take heart because Christ, Himself, prayed, 'My God, my God, why hast thou forsaken me?'"[1]

Elton Trueblood

Have you ever noticed how problems appear more manageable in daylight than in the darkness? How pain is more bearable in the daytime than in the night? There's something about darkness that exaggerates problems and exacerbates pain.

At noon, after Jesus had hung on the Cross since nine o'clock, a thick darkness settled over the earth. In the awful darkness, Jesus cried out in a loud voice, *Eloi, Eloi, lama sabachthani?* which means, "My God, my God, why have you forsaken me?" (Mark 15:33–34 NIV).

How could Jesus, the Son of God who was doing God's will, feel abandoned? And if He was forsaken, does this mean God might forsake us? What encouragement, if any, does this mysterious prayer have for those of us trying to come to terms with things we can't change?

Jesus' mysterious prayer

If we take the prayer at face value, the prayer represents a response of despair to severe testing. Many Bible interpreters cannot fathom Jesus making this kind of response. The words of this prayer are taken directly from Psalm 22:1, so some say Jesus was quoting it in confidence and trust as death neared. Psalm 22 begins in despair and ends on a triumphant note, but many psalms have the same pattern. I am inclined to agree with William Barclay, who says, "On a cross a man does not repeat poetry to himself, even the poetry of a psalm."[2]

Other Bible scholars say Jesus felt forsaken because He was bearing the sins of the world. Up to this moment Jesus had gone through every experience of life except one: being separated from God because of sin. Jesus had taken this life of ours upon Himself. He had done our work and faced our temptations and borne our trials. He had suffered all that life could bring to Him. He had known the failure of friends, the hatred of foes, the malice of enemies, but He had never known the consequence of sin because He was without sin.

Sin separates us from God. It puts between God and us a barrier that is like an unscalable wall. Jesus had never experienced this separation because He was without sin. When Jesus hung on the Cross, identifying Himself with the sin of humanity (2 Corinthians 5:21), He felt what it was like to be separated from God by sin.

This experience must have been agonizing for Him because He had never known this kind of separation. On the Cross, He felt passing over Him the awful loneliness of a soul separated from God, and His prayer expressed the wretchedness of what that was like.

Elton Trueblood sees loneliness as an explanation for Jesus' mysterious prayer. In his book *The Lord's Prayers*, he writes that the loneliness he experienced must have been almost unbearable. It is true that we often count on the support of fellow believers to help us through difficult times. We credit their support as God's doing; His way of letting us know He is with us. When we don't have that kind of support, loneliness engulfs us. Jesus had little support at the Cross. Trueblood states, "The crowd, instead of being moved to compassion by His suffering, were either idly curious or openly glad that He was in torment. Instead of compassion, which He needed at this point, He received ridicule."[3]

Jesus was scoffed at by the crowd and the soldiers. Some women followers stood at a distance, but where were the apostles? Where were the ones He had given His closest attention? Where were Peter and James, members of His inner circle, with whom He had shared His glory on the Mountain of Transfiguration and His agony in Gethsemane? The darkness accentuated His loneliness. To be in the midst of people and not be able to sense that others know, or care to know, what is happening to you is a loneliness that makes you feel abandoned by God.

I believe pain could be another possible explanation (or a part of the explanation) for His cry of abandonment. Long iron nails were driven between the bones of His wrists into the wooden crossbar. The nails usually tore through the median nerve. This would have created an unending trail of fire up His arms, augmenting the pain from the long spike through

His ankles. The rigidity of his position caused muscle cramps. Dehydration created intense thirst.

Jesus was already so weak from the whipping He received preceding the Crucifixion that the Roman soldiers had to tap Simon of Cyrene to carry His Cross (Luke 23:26; Mark 15:21). Now, nailed to the Cross, He couldn't even swipe at the gnats and flies that swarmed around the dried blood on His head and back. He couldn't wipe the sweat from His forehead. He was experiencing a degree of agony exceeding that of Gethsemane.

Excruciating pain for hours at a time can make a person feel abandoned by God, as many cancer patients will tell you. To me, it takes nothing away from Jesus' humanity—or His divinity—if He cried out because of the physical torture of the Crucifixion. If His pain reached the point of making Him feel abandoned by God, that makes His sacrifice (and love) for me all the greater.

Perhaps the explanation for Jesus' mysterious prayer isn't one of these, but all of them. The spiritual, emotional, and physical ramifications of the Cross pressed in on Him. In the darkness they were magnified in such a way as to make Him feel abandoned. He expressed His forsakenness with a scriptural prayer.

Many of life's experiences, especially those in which we feel forsaken by God, are not neat and tidy. Many variables enter the picture. They overlap and interlace in such a way that we end up feeling isolated and confused.

Multiple reasons, multiple hurts

When I am asked why I became depressed, I answer, "A loss of purpose." While that was the bottom line of my depression, other variables were involved.

- The many rejections we received when Bob tried to enter the ministry, even from our own church. Too much of my self-esteem was wrapped up in what other Christians thought of me.
- I'm a ruminator, and people with ruminating response styles are more prone to depression. Ruminating serves me well as a writer and Bible teacher, but it fueled the fire of depression as I reviewed over and over again what had happened to us.
- I held in my despair over the past and anxiety over the future. Unexpressed emotion provides fertile ground for growing depression.

People dealing with disappointments often find themselves with diminished physical strength. The hardest time for me was late in the afternoons, when I experienced what I called the "four o'clock blues." This was also when I was tired from the day's work and was trying to fix dinner for the family.

EVENTUALLY I SOUGHT professional help for my depression and made good progress. The physical symptoms went away but those pesky four o'clock blues didn't. Confusion would roll in and the sadness of depression would cover me.

One afternoon, I was peeling potatoes when the sadness descended. I thought, *I've got to do something about this.* I put down my paring knife and went to the bathroom. With the door locked, I knelt by the tub and cried, "God, how could you do this to us? How could you hurt us when we've tried so hard to serve you?" Without realizing it, Jesus' cry from the Cross had been imprinted on my mind as I studied His prayer life. I prayed His prayer just as He had prayed the psalmist's prayer. The emotional intensity of praying that afternoon surprised me. As the tears flowed, I cried over and over again, "How could You do this to us?" I had held and packed in the hurt for so long that when I let it go, the emotion gushed forth.

After a while, the tears subsided, and I felt some relief. The dark cloud of sadness lifted. I got up, washed my face, and returned to the kitchen. The next afternoon, around four o'clock, the cloud returned. It wasn't as ominous this time, but it was back. I returned to the bathroom altar and prayed again, "How could you do this to us?" The praying wasn't quite as intense this time. There were fewer tears, and again I gained some relief. The cloud dissipated and I returned to preparing dinner.

Would you believe that the next afternoon the cloud was back hovering over me? This may give you the impression that honest praying wasn't working, but it was. After a few afternoons of praying this way, the four o'clock blues ceased, and what was even more important, I no longer felt abandoned by God.

In the days ahead, I felt stronger, more able to handle life. Nothing about our situation had changed, but my vision had improved. The future no longer looked dismal. The difference was so profound that I was glad I had instinctively known (from studying Jesus' prayer life) that I could ask God why. His cry from the Cross reminds us that we who struggle with things we can't change may ask why and find relief and reassurance.

Permission to ask

Jesus did not fail in being obedient to God, yet He dared to ask why. He did not curse God like His neighbor on the cross.

But He questioned Him. And that is a comfort to those of us who may also wonder why. When we are sincerely baffled by what we are experiencing, His example gives us permission to ask which is what Harold Myra did.

In his book *Surprised by Children*, Myra tells how his parents cared for several foster children who came from terrible circumstances. One of them, Richie, was with his parents for seven years and made a faith commitment before being returned to his biological mother. A few years later, Richie murdered Mrs. Prosser, a neighbor to Myra's parents.

Myra was baffled by this. How could this be? His mother had reached out to Richie, nurtured him, introduced him to Christ's love, and he had been responding before returning to his mother. Myra wondered how he could be pulled away from the truth and resort to something so devastating.

His mind was in turmoil. His thoughts rumbled and ruptured into a complaint to God. Seeing Richie as trapped and doomed, Myra tearfully said, "How could you do this? . . . Lord, how can you run your world with such capricious horror?" [4]

Myra said that God's response was clear:

> *"I'm not upset by your prayers." On the contrary, it was as if God had been waiting for me to look evil full in the face and confront him.*
>
> *God seemed to say, "How do you think I feel about Richie? About Mrs. Prosser? Haven't I wept over them? Haven't I sent my Son to die for them?"*
>
> *This flowed into me as a personal, forceful connection with God. I sensed that he was drawing me into his perspective, that he was calling me almost as a colleague to join forces in extending his love, to intercede for others in their helplessness—and that he was indeed in charge, transcending all tragedies.* [5]

God's response

Asking why doesn't necessarily mean we will receive an answer that explains why we are experiencing what we are. It may happen, but it may not. We may not receive an explanation in the here and now. What we will receive is more likely to be a spiritual result something like one of these:

- A lightening of the burden we carry.
- A clearing in our inner space, giving God room to work.
- A winding down of strong emotions because asking why may be an emotional release as much as it is a question.
- Receiving a personal, forceful connection with God as Myra did.
- Feeling hopeful about the future, not mired in the past any longer.
- Reassurance that we aren't forsaken. The feeling of abandonment will cease.

While we may have felt forsaken, the Bible assures us that God will never leave us or forsake us (Deuteronomy 31:6; Joshua 1:5; Hebrews 13:5). That's true even though we sometimes feel forsaken. God doesn't abandon us, and He didn't abandon Jesus.

God was there

While Jesus felt forsaken, events around the Cross reveal that God did not abandon Him.

The supernatural darkness. What nature did at this time shows us God's heart. Jesus' death was so terrible that the sky was unnaturally darkened, as if nature could not bear to look.

The darkness was not due to an eclipse because it was the time of the full moon of Passover week. The "simplest explanation is that it was a supernatural manifestation in nature . . . in sympathy with the crucial experience through which nature's Maker was passing during those three hours." [6]

Death came in a short time. Because no major organs were affected, crucifixion was usually a slow death. It sometimes took days. Jesus died in six hours. It was as if God were saying, "The Cross may be necessary, but I'll not have you suffer any longer than is necessary."

Shout of triumph. After His cry of abandonment, Jesus gave a victorious shout (Matthew 27:50; Mark 15:37; Luke 23:46): "It is finished" (John 19:30). In the Greek, that would have been one word: *Finished!* It was the shout of a man who had completed the task, a man who had won through the struggle, a man who had come out of darkness into light. Jesus died with the cry of triumph on His lips, His task accomplished, His work completed, His victory won.

The temple veil was split. God responded as a Jewish father would at the death of a child. When Jacob saw the multicolored coat of his beloved Joseph drenched in blood, he rent his garment as an expression of deepest sorrow. When Job got the shocking news of the death of his children, he tore his clothes as a symbol of his anguish. When Jesus died, God rent the temple curtain from top to bottom, symbolically revealing His heart of sorrow and love.

Taken together, these events tell us that God did not forsake Jesus. He had been close by during the whole, terrible ordeal. God was there. And this should console us during times when we *feel* forsaken and alone. The fact is we are not abandoned; how do we translate that fact into feeling? The same way Jesus did: through honest praying.

Asking why is not an everyday kind of prayer. We wouldn't want to turn into believers who are always wringing their hands, bemoaning their fate, and continuing to question God. After all, we walk in faith, but this prayer experience of Jesus' reminds that there are times when we are truly perplexed, when we do indeed feel forsaken. This is when it is time to pray Jesus' prayer of abandonment.

When we do not understand, when we cannot see how God could possibly be at work in our circumstances, then we can pray as Jesus prayed, "My God, my God, why have you forsaken me?" What I hope you will discover is what I discovered: God was there all the time.

From inspiration to application

How is Jesus' cry of abandonment from the Cross both awful and consoling?

What is one way I can express my feelings of abandonment?

What will I discover when I honestly express what I am feeling and thinking?

"Save me, O God!
The water is up to my neck;
I am sinking in deep mud,
And there is no solid ground;
I am out in deep water;
And the waves are about to drown me.
I am worn out from calling for help." [7]

Part III

The Resolution
Release and Peace

*"Unless a grain of wheat
falls into the ground and dies,
it remains a single grain.
But if it does die,
it yields a great harvest."*

John 12:24 (Williams)

Chapter 16

Into Thy Hands

"Here's something you can't dream your way out of, I told myself. Here's something you can't think your way out of, buy your way out of, or work your way out of. It was all too clear. ... This is, I thought to myself, something you can only trust your way out of." [1]

Bob Buford, in response to his son's death

At God's direction, Mark (from chaps. 1 and 2) enrolled in a community college after being fired from his book-selling job. Uncertain, at first, what his new career would be, he began with computer courses—programming and maintenance as well as application courses. He had used computers for years, but now he enjoyed learning the behind-the-activity part of computers. Soon he was hooked. He got a part-time job with a computer business while he finished his degree in computer technology.

The week after he graduated, his boss hired him to manage the business. Mark couldn't have been happier. He was so glad he didn't have to travel any more. One evening over coffee, he said to his wife, "Being fired was one of the best things that ever happened to me."

Six years after the Christian university told Bob they would not renew his contract, we received a call from Bill, a pastor friend in another state. The previous Sunday, Bill had been absent from his pulpit and had asked a Christian college president to fill in for him. When Bill got back to his office, he played the tape of the president's message. The president had said they were looking for people to fill two administrative positions they had open.

Knowing our situation, Bill called immediately. He was so excited. He said, "I think this is it."

And it was. Bob wrote the college for a job description, applied, and in a few months had one of the jobs. What happened to us was like a peculiar parenthesis. As suddenly as the bizarre job difficulties started, they ended, and my husband became employed as a college administrator once again.

The way Mark's and Bob's stories end is how we would like all of our stories to end. We would like our struggle with what we can't change to make sense like Mark's did. We would like to think that our own parenthesis in life will close as Bob's did. We like satisfying endings. Unfortunately, our stories may end differently.

Even when we pray Jesus' way, our situation may still not make sense. We can withdraw to lonely places, we can express gratitude and we can be honest about our emotions, and still not have that sense of rightness that Mark experienced. This doesn't take anything away from the relief the tools bring. They enable us to cope even when the "why" escapes us.

Some situations defy an explanation—at least, in this life. Edmund was 26 years old when he was diagnosed with amyotrophic lateral sclerosis (ALS or Lou Gehrig's disease). His neurologist told him, "You have 6 to 12 months to live." Death was inevitable. Sitting in his wheelchair day after day, Edmund wondered, *Why me? I'm too young to have my life end. This doesn't make any sense.*

In cases like Edmund's, we think of all we wanted in life. We become preoccupied with "what might have been" or "what never will be." We stew over what appears to be God's unfairness.

Even when we pray Jesus' way, our situation may not be reversible, where we can go back to the way things were. The limb that was amputated cannot be sewed back on, the eye that was lost cannot be replaced, and the child who died will not be coming back. While we may be coping outwardly, inwardly we may become resentful. We make a partial adjustment using Jesus' tools, but not a complete adjustment. A dark residue lingers, robbing us of inner peace.

For those whose situation doesn't make sense, is unexplainable or irreversible, there remains a final application from Jesus' prayer life that will help. It has to do with trusting God with what we cannot change.

"Into Thy Hands . . ."

After His prayer of abandonment on the Cross, after making arrangements for His mother's care, "Jesus knew that by now everything had been completed" (John 19:28). Jesus said, "It is finished!" (v. 30). All that Jesus had done, sought, hoped for, loved, and dreamed were finished. He had accomplished what the Father called Him to do. His work was finished. All that He could do had been done; all that He could give had been given. And after Jesus had loudly cried, "It is finished!" He said, "Father, into thy hands I commend my spirit: and having said thus, he gave up the ghost" (Luke 23:46 KJV).

From His first prayer, He knew His mission and His destiny, and He could die knowing He had achieved what God wanted Him to achieve. "Here, Father, I give You my life. I give You My work."

When we've done all we can do about our situation, when we have wrestled with it and lost sleep over it, we can give it to God. It's the attitude—the trust inherent in Jesus' prayer—that we want to emulate.

The prayer of trust

Commend means to entrust, to deliver with confidence, to give as a deposit for trust or safekeeping. Jesus' obedience all through His life had been a lovely thing, and now even though He experienced the Cross and the feeling of abandonment, He deposited His life into the hands of God.

The words of Jesus' prayer come from Psalm 31:5 (KJV): "Into thine hand I commit my spirit." Jews often used this phrase as a prayer by adding the word, "Father." It was the first prayer every Jewish mother taught her child to say when he lay down to sleep at night, before the threatening dark came. Perhaps Mary had taught this prayer to Jesus. When He was dying, Jesus prayed the prayer He had prayed many times as a little boy.

Following the prayer, Jesus bowed His head and died. The Gospel writer John says that Jesus leaned back His head and gave up His spirit. The word that John uses is the word that might be used for settling back upon a pillow. For Jesus the strife was over; the battle was won. So there came to Jesus the peace after His long battle, rest after His earnest work, and contentment knowing He had completed His task. With the sure and restful sigh of a tried child, He died confident of His Father's care. He no longer felt forsaken.

This peace is what we want, isn't it? I know it is what I want. I want to be confident of the Father's care and to be able to rest in Him. I want whatever inner agitation I'm experiencing about what I can't change to cease, and I found it will when I adopt the trustful attitude inherent in Jesus' final prayer. Sometimes this is easy, and sometimes it isn't.

When a simple prayer will do

For some, placing what they can't change in God's hands may come simply and easily—once they recognize the need for it. It did for 45-year-old Jill (from chap. 1) who was so resistant to aging. Jill dyed her hair, dressed youthfully, watched her weight, and exercised rigorously to look young. Nevertheless, ageism comments still bothered her, particularly jokes about older people. One distasteful joke about an old woman could put her in a bad mood for days. One day as Jill thought about this while bike riding, it occurred to her that she had another option; she could accept her age and learn to live with it. "Father," she prayed, "aging is a part of Your design. I accept it and I give You my concerns about it."

To verify her acceptance, she rode to the youth director's office. She said to Tom, "I have a confession to make. I can't help you with chaperoning any more because I'm not under 40. I'm 45, soon to be 46."

Tom looked embarrassed. He said, "I'm sorry I made that announcement about chaperones having to be under 40. Groping for words to attract people with a youthful attitude,

I said the wrong thing. I've regretted it ever since. We want you for a chaperone, and we need you."

When it's more complicated

For some, a one-time prayer like Jill prayed will not be enough to deposit our circumstances into God's hands. We may not have her trusting nature. Our situation may be so difficult that we look at hers and think, What's aging compared to my problem? Jesus' prayer was one of genuine trust in God. It was not a prayer of resignation, "OK, God, you win." Arriving at trust like Jesus exhibited will not come effortlessly for many of us. It may be as difficult as praying for God to forgive those who have wronged us (chap. 14). There's no quick fix, but there are some prayer exercises we can do to aid the process.

We may need to start with our lack of trust. If we have been truly shocked by what happened to us, or if it seemed out of line with our concept of God, we may find ourselves reluctant to trust Him. Or, our pain may be so bad we question whether God cares. We may have to begin the depositing process by confessing our lack of trust: "Father, I've been deeply hurt by what happened. I want to trust you again, but I am afraid to. I give you my fear so that I can eventually give you what I can't change."

We may need to pray Jesus' prayer of commitment over and over to develop trust. We may need to make it a part of our regular prayers. A woman whose husband was mentally ill said, "My experience has been that acceptance comes as a daily decision, much like setting the thermostat in the living room. It's something I must do over and over again."

A close friend does this with regard to her fear of death—the unchangeable we all face. She told me, "Sometimes when

I think about death I feel all claustrophobic—truly like I'm in a vise. I want to push against reality closing in and make it not be true. When this fear surrounds me, I wrestle with it, and I pray, 'Father, into thy hands I commend my spirit.'" I usually have to do this over several days before inner peace returns. Then life will plateau for a while—for months or sometimes years I will not think about death, and then the fear returns. That's when I start repeating Jesus' prayer of commitment. Sometimes I underscore it at night before going to sleep with a child's version, 'If I should die before I wake, I pray the Lord my soul to take.' Life is fuller and more blessed—and I'm happier—when I chose to use Jesus' prayer to deal with the inevitability of death."

Just as Jesus used the words of a psalmist, we may need to use someone else's words like my friend used a child's prayer. We could paraphrase Jesus' prayer: "I have done all I can do. My efforts are exhausted. I give—I relinquish—the situation to you. With childlike trust I deposit my situation in your hands." Or we could adapt E. Stanley Jones's prayer: "I am Yours and this thing concerns me, and so this is Yours, too. I surrender it to You." [2]

We may need to break down what we can't change into portions and give God one portion at a time. Tina discovered this when she was diagnosed with rheumatoid arthritis. She said, "I was filled with sadness. With this affliction, I had lost my career, my control over my life, my future as I had envisioned it, and my sense of wellness. I had to let each of these go, one by one committing them to God. This was difficult for me but as I did, God responded with gifts of comfort and peace. The sadness left, and eventually, with God's help, I learned to live with what I couldn't change."

We may need to do something that signifies the fact that we have given our situation to God. For example, imagine what you can't change as a burden you are holding in your hand, much the same way you would hold a basketball or a bowl of fruit. As you talk to God about the burden, as you "see" it before you, sense its heaviness. After telling Him about it, hand over the burden to Him (extend your hands upward or outward). Handing it to Him, say, "Here I give it to You. I can no longer carry it."

Similarly, you might want to write about your burden on a piece of paper. Afterwards, burn the paper or tear it up in tiny pieces and release it to the wind: "I trust my burden to You; it is no longer mine."

Or better yet, hold a grain of wheat or a seed of some kind in your hand. Visualize the seed as whatever it is that you can't change. Bury it in the ground, symbolizing the burial of your resistance to accepting your situation. Watch for it to grow day by day and expect to reap the harvest Jesus alluded to in John 12:24. As you watch, verbally affirm what God is going to do: "Father, I have buried what I cannot change; I look forward to seeing this seed sprout and grow. I look forward to the harvest you are going to give me."

Planting a seed is a good description of trust. When a farmer drops a seed into the ground, it becomes warm and begins to grow. When we deposit the seed depicting what we can't change into God's care, He warms it and makes it grow.

In a way, for some, what we can't change is a like a precious heirloom seed. We want to hold on to it, preserve it, keep it so we take special care of it; we're reluctant to plant it in the ground. As long as we do, peace will elude us. We must open our hands that clutch our treasured seed before our hands can be free to hold something else. Once we accept what we cannot change, then we can use our time and our energy to focus on what we can change and what we can do. We can focus on living life fully.

What we can do

A hospice doctor encouraged Edmund to accept his inevitable death. While Edmund believed in a life after death, it was the loss of the "now" that bothered him. The doctor helped him to see that the "now" still had potential. The doctor said, "Your muscles are atrophying, but you still have your mind, and you still have your verbal abilities. Use them. Record your history of what you are going through, what you are thinking and feeling, as this disease progresses. This history can be used to help others who suffer from the same disease."

When our focus shifts from what we have lost to what we have, from what we can't change to what we can, then we know we have accepted our situation. The inner wrestling is replaced by inner peace. The agitation ceases. Calmness returns to our spirit as we are freed of the strife that continually robbed us of inner harmony. Not everyone's unchangeable can have a glorious ending, but they can all have a peaceful ending.

From inspiration to application

What might I need to relinquish in order to experience peace and serenity?

How will accepting what I cannot change enable me to see what I can change?

What are some ways I can deposit what I cannot change into God's hands?

"In thee, O Lord, do I put my trust. . . .
Into thine hand I commit my spirit." [3]

Chapter 17

Release from the Vise

"No matter what happens to us, we hold in our hearts the joy of the Lord, submerged at times by pain or adversity, but always deep within our beings. We may indeed suffer, but He was crucified and yet rose again. No matter what happens to us, we know that beyond the Cross lies the Resurrection." [1]

Emily Gardiner Neal

When I asked Russ (from chap. 1) what was the most difficult part of dealing with Sara's accident and injuries, he said, "The feeling of helplessness. There is no way I can fix the physical scars Sara has suffered."

This feeling of helplessness is what makes "being in a vise" an apt description of what we can't change. Caught in its jaws, we feel like there's nothing we can do, but that just isn't true. We can pray like Jesus prayed.

Lessons from Jesus' prayer life

We can take the various lessons we have learned from studying Jesus' prayer life and apply them to our particular situations.

We can visit lonely places. We can imitate Jesus' deliberate withdrawals to be alone with God. In solitude, God can refresh, strengthen, and guide us. We can align our will with God's will so we may stay on track as believers.

We can express gratitude as Jesus did. We can do so during bright shining moments and during the difficult times too. Allan (from chap. 1) discovered this after his wife, Ruth, died. "In every thing give thanks: for this is the will of God in Christ Jesus concerning you" (1 Thessalonians 5:18 NASB) became embedded in his mind. Allan said, "I couldn't seem to shake it or replace it with anything else. I had not been reading in 1 Thessalonians at the time, but it seemed that this was the message the Lord had for me." Indeed it was, because giving thanks enabled Allan to cope. He counted himself a fortunate man as he appreciated the kind of woman Ruth was, the number of years they were married, and the two fine daughters they had raised. He said, "God couldn't have given me a more appropriate word."

We can honestly express our emotions. In Jesus' praying, there was no pretense, no cover-up, no repression of feelings. In front of a group of people, as He headed toward Jerusalem and the Cross, He said, "Now is my soul troubled" (John 12:27). Deeply distressed and full of anguish, Jesus acknowledged, "My soul is overwhelmed with sorrow" (Mark 14:34; Matthew 26:38 NIV) when He prayed for an escape from the Cross. On the Cross, Jesus cried, "My God, my God, why hast thou forsaken me?" (Mark 15:34). Honest praying gave God a channel for ministering to His needs, and honest praying will do the same for us.

We can adopt Jesus' attitude of trust and confidence by giving God what we can't change. Through any number of prayer exercises, we can deposit what we can't change into God's hands the way a gardener buries a seed. Putting the seed into the ground implies a willingness to let go. Covering it with dirt says, "I'm taking my hands off and leaving it to you." Standing up, patting the dirt with our foot, and looking at the horizon says, "I can't wait to see what this grain will eventually produce." This action exemplifies the prophet Habakkuk's stance. He said, "I will climb my watchtower and wait to see what the Lord will tell me to say and what answer he will give to my complaint" (Habakkuk 2:1).

We can rely on Jesus' intercession. As we walked with Jesus from His baptism to the Cross, we learned how much effort He put into His prayer life. Praying about what we can't change is neither simple or easy. As Allan related, "If ever there was a time in my life that I didn't feel like giving thanks, it was after Ruth's death. I had just been deprived of the companionship of the one person who meant more to me than life itself, and being thankful was hardly what I was experiencing."

If we are honest, we may be just as skeptical as Allan was about praying Jesus' way. Or we may become too exhausted to pray. Our faith may weaken, or we may be in too much pain to concentrate. Our fears may overwhelm us. At those times, we can be comforted in knowing that Jesus is interceding on our behalf. What Jesus did for Peter and for His disciples, He does for us in His perpetual role as intercessor.

We can count on God to answer us. Even though many of the answers Jesus received to His prayers didn't spell "end of struggle," God always answered Jesus.

When Jesus wanted to know if His disciples were beginning to grasp who He was, Jesus prayed. In response, God provided Peter's confession, "You are the Christ" (Matthew 16:16 NIV).

When Jesus realized His time was limited and He needed to choose men to train to carry on His ministry, He spent the night praying. By morning He had His answer. He called His disciples to Him and chose 12 of them to be His apostles to carry on His ministry after He was gone.

When the disciples didn't understand the nature of Jesus' ministry and when Jesus Himself needed confirmation, God responded with the transfiguration experience.

After Jesus prayed, "Now is my soul troubled," God gave Him strength to go on to Jerusalem toward the Cross.

After His plea for escape in the Garden of Gethsemane, God strengthened Jesus in such a way that He proceeded calmly and resolutely toward the Cross. Throughout the arrest and His trials, Jesus—more than Pilate, more than those who sought His arrest—appeared to be in control.

After His cry of abandonment from the Cross, fellowship between the Father and the Son was restored, Jesus died with a shout of triumph on His lips and with the confidence of a child falling asleep in his father's arms.

We can trust God to respond in the same way to us. His answers will be sufficient when we follow Jesus' example, pray the way He did, and come to accept what we can't change.

Resulting benefits

What many of us were looking for when we decided to walk with Jesus from His baptism to the Cross was the ability to cope with what we can't change. Our only thought might have been, If I can just get through this, and that is what praying Jesus' way will do for us. It will enable us to cope, yet it does more than that. The seed that dies "produces many grains" (John 12:24).

Release from the vise. When we pattern our prayer life after Jesus', the vise's grip will be released. All along we felt the grip was outside of us, as if there were actually a large physical vise holding us against our will, pressing in on us. Yet when we deposit what we can't change into God's hands, then we discover that the vise was on the inside where it affected our outlook and held our energy hostage. Released from the vise's grip, we feel free—and we are. We are no longer in bondage to what we can't change.

Peace prevails. Jesus said, "Take my yoke upon you and learn from me" (Matthew 11:29 NIV). When we identify with Jesus, learn from Him and imitate Him, we receive rest for our souls (v. 29*b*). The agitation winds itself down. The anxiety over what we can't change ceases.

Joy surfaces. I once disagreed with a Sunday School teacher who said that Jesus always experienced joy. I said, "Not on the Cross." I cannot see joy coexisting within someone who feels so abandoned He cries out, "My God, my God, why have you forsaken me?"

All of us from time to time go through periods where the joy of the Lord and/or the joy of living are submerged by pain or adversity. When we truly accept what we can't change, joy returns to our spirit and strengthens us.

Focus changes. Once Joni (in chap. 3) identified with Jesus, she learned from Him how to deal with what she could not change. Once she felt a kinship with Him, she said, "My focus changed from demanding an explanation from God to humbly depending on Him."[2] In this position, God could respond to her and help her.

Perspective changes. To understand the illness of depression, I began studying it. What I learned about depression was so insightful that I wrote a book on understanding a woman's depression. When a psychiatrist's secretary read it, she said, "You are right on target. You know women, and you know the subject of depression."

Pleased with her comments, I started singing along with the car radio as I drove. While singing, I mused over what Bob and I had been through. In my musing, I thought I heard the words, *God meant it for my good.*

I shook my head, trying to clear my mind.

The words came again: *God meant it for my good.*

I turned off the radio, and in the quiet I heard the words again: *God meant it for my good.*

Hadn't Joseph said something similar to that after he reconciled with his brothers who sold him into slavery (Genesis 50:20)? When I checked the reference, a window in my soul opened. I could see better, and I felt a lightness in my spirit. The depression no longer seemed like an awful black pit; rather, it seemed to be a passage leading to a new life, and indeed it has been that. I grew and gained from the experience.

Personal growth. In researching depression, I learned about the power the subconscious can have over the conscious. I learned what it means to be a woman, and that knowledge helped me begin to live in harmony with myself. I learned I responded to life's problems by ruminating and that I had faulty thinking patterns like overgeneralizing and taking things personally. What I learned was so life changing that

I would hate to think what my life would be like today if I hadn't changed. While I would never want to be depressed again, I have to admit it was one of the best things that ever happened to me.

Peggy, from chapter 1, agrees. She says, "I can truthfully say scleroderma is the worst thing and the best thing that has ever happened to me. It is the worse because it is a devastating illness. It is the best because it made me run to my Lord with my arms empty but open wide. He has lovingly helped me look at my life and my death, my gifts and my limitations, my hopes and my fears, and most importantly, He taught me to keep my focus on Him and Him alone . . . I wouldn't turn down the gift of physical healing in the future, but I also wouldn't give up one thing He has taught me through having to deal with scleroderma."

Every grief and disappointment we have is an opportunity for us to learn some new truth, to open some new door to a larger life, to discover new dimensions of wholeness, meaning, joy and love.

Growing closer to Christ. The best part for me was coming to know Jesus better. When I took hold of His hand and began walking with Him toward the Cross, I identified with Him. We were—and still are—in life's struggle together. I began to see Him as someone to learn from. His example in prayer became indelibly printed on my mind; I've applied what I've learned over and over again. In the "fellowship of his sufferings," my life became intertwined with His.

Being fully alive. With some things that we can't change, it would be easy to begin to see ourselves as a victim and grow resentful and bitter. On the other hand, when we work through our emotions and deposit what we can't change into God's hands, we become intensely aware of the present and the blessings around us.

As Gerald Sittser adjusted to the deaths of his wife, his mother, and his daughter, he wrote,

> *I was struck by how wonderful ordinary life is. Simply being alive became holy to me. As I saw myself typing exams, chatting with a student on the way to class, or tucking one of my children into bed, I sensed I was beholding something sacred.* [3]

The light of the Resurrection

While Jesus' prayers must always be interpreted in light of the Cross, the Cross must always be interpreted in light of the Resurrection. Jesus did not stay on the Cross. Release from His long struggle came in the form of the Resurrection, giving purpose and meaning to all He had been through.

If we follow Jesus' way of praying, release will come for us too. There will come a resurrection in our lives—a time when we are free from the vise and are ready to embrace life again. When we truly accept what we can't change, everything changes.

From inspiration to application

Of the many lessons from Jesus' prayer life, which one was the most insightful to me?

What benefits can I expect to experience when I pattern my prayer life after Jesus'?

What changes when I accept what I cannot change?

"O Joy that seekest me through pain,
I cannot close my heart to thee;
I trace the rainbow thro' the rain." [4]

Endnotes

Chapter 1

[1]William Barclay, *The Daily Study Bible*, vol. 2, *The Revelation of John* (Edinburgh, Scotland: The Saint Andrew Press, 1965), 32.
[2]From the old hymn, "O Love That Wilt Not Let Me Go," words by George Matheson, 1842–1906.

Chapter 2

[1]John Claypool, *Glad Reunion* (Waco, TX: Word Books, 1984), 135.
[2]Rebecca Manley Pippert, *Hope Has Its Reasons* (New York: Harper and Row, 1989), 191.
[3]Ibid.
[4]Ray Summers, *Commentary on Luke* (Waco, TX: Word Books, 1972), 43.

Chapter 3

[1]Elton Trueblood, *The Lord's Prayers* (New York, Evanston, and London: Harper and Row, 1965), 17.
[2]Kenneth S. Wuest, *Wuest's Word Studies: First Peter in the Greek New Testament* (Grand Rapids, MI: William B. Eerdmans Publishing Company, 1942), 67.
[3]Philip Yancey, *Where Is God When It Hurts?* (Grand Rapids, MI: Zondervan Publishing House, 1977), 118–19.
[4]Mark 9:24 (KJV).

Chapter 4

[1]Halford E. Luccock, *The Interpreter's Bible*, vol. 7 (Nashville: Abingdon Press, 1955), 666.

[2]If you have read *Can Martha Have a Mary Christmas?*, you will remember that I used this same illustration to explain the concept of getting to know Christ and to experience him.

[3]I have posted a free study exercise entitled Jesus' Inferred Prayers on Scribd.com. You may use this exercise to draw your own conclusions and see whether you agree with mine. Either way, the exercise will be beneficial in helping you identify with Jesus and draw closer to him.

[4]For this book, I used A. T. Robertson's *A Harmony of the Gospels for Students of the Life of Christ* (New York: Harper and Brothers Publishers, 1950) to determine the chronology of Jesus' prayers.

[5]Psalm 5:3 (NIV).

Chapter 5

[1]Donald Zochert, *Laura: The Life of Laura Ingalls Wilder* (Chicago: Contemporary Books, Inc., 1976), 225–26.

[2]William Barclay, *The Daily Study Bible*, vol. 1, *The Gospel of Matthew*, 6th imp. (Edinburgh, Scotland: The Saint Andrew Press, 1965), 304.

[3]Gerald L. Sittser, *A Grace Disguised* (Grand Rapids, MI: Zondervan Publishing House, 1996), 34.

[4]Ibid., 35.

[5]David Hazard, "Listening in Silence," *Charisma*, July 1996, 63.

[6]*The Interpreter's Bible*, vol. 8 (Nashville: Abingdon Press, 1955), 104.

[7]From the old hymn "Open My Eyes That I May See," words by Clara H. Scott, 1841–97.

Chapter 6

[1]Brainy Quote, "Louisa May Alcott Quotes," http://www
.brainyquote.com/quotes/authors/l/louisa_may_alcott
(accessed March 25, 2013).
[2]Elton Trueblood, *The Lord's Prayers* (New York, Evanston,
and London: Harper and Row, 1965), 39.
[3]Ibid.
[4]Acts 9:6.

Chapter 7

[1]William Barclay, *The Daily Study Bible*, vol. 2, *The Revelation of John* (Edinburgh, Scotland: The Saint Andrew Press,
1965), 127.
[2]From the old hymn, "I'll Live for Him," words by Ralph E.
Hudson, 1843–1901.

Chapter 8

[1]Harry Emerson Fosdick, *The Meaning of Prayer* (New York:
Association Press, 1915), 130.
[2]William Barclay, *The Mind of Jesus* (New York: Harper and
Row, 1960, 1961), 167.
[3]Fosdick, *The Meaning of Prayer*, 130.
[4]Ibid., 130–1.
[5]Hebrews 13:20–21 (NCV); pronoun "you" changed to "me"
by author for this prayer.

Chapter 9
[1]B. H. Carroll, *Messages on Prayer*, comp. J. W. Crowder, ed.
J. B. Cranfill (Nashville: Broadman Press, 1942), 41.
[2]J. W. Shepard, *The Christ of the Gospels: An Exegetical Study*

(Grand Rapids, MI: William. B. Eerdmans Publishing Company, 1956), 315.

[3]William Barclay, *The Mind of Jesus* (New York: Harper and Row, 1960, 1961), 180–81,

[4]Carroll, *Messages on Prayer*, 40.

[5]From the old hymn, "Christ, Whose Glory Fills the Skies," words by Charles Wesley.

Chapter 10

[1]John P. Newport, *The Lion and the Lamb* (Nashville: Broadman Press, 1986), 173.

[2]Habakkuk 3:18 (NIV); Matthew 11:26 (KJV).

Chapter 11

[1]Luke 12:49–50 (TLB).

[2]The sequence of the selected scenes is based on A. T. Robertson's *Harmony of the Gospels for Students of the Life of Christ.* The dialogue in the scenes is not verbatim from the Bible; rather, it is the author's version of what could have been said based on the biblical accounts.

[3]Psalm 25:17 (KJV).

Chapter 12

[1]Romans 8:34, 35, 37; author's italics.

[2]Christians differ on the rightness or wrongness of praying to Jesus and to the Holy Spirit.
For a discussion on this topic, see chapter 8 of Brenda Poinsett's book, *Prayerfully Yours* (Nashville: Broadman Press, 1979).

[3]Psalm 110:4.

[4]From the old hymn, "Hail, Thou Once Despised Jesus," words by John Bakewell, 1721–1819.

Chapter 13

[1]Paul Thigpen, "Losing and Finding My Father," *Charisma* and *Christian Life*, June 1990.
[2]William Barclay, *The Daily Study Bible, The Gospel of Luke*, 3rd ed. (Edinburgh, Scotland: The Saint Andrew Press, 1964), 283.
[3]Ronald Dunn, *When Heaven Is Silent* (Nashville: Thomas Nelson Publishers, 1994), 131.
[4]John M. Koessler, "Keys to a Healthy Emotional Life," *Decision*, September 1991, 27.
[5]Ibid.
[6]Karen Burton Mains, *Karen! Karen!* (Wheaton, IL: Tyndale House Publishers, Inc., 1979), 54.
[7]Frank Maier and Ginny Maier, *Sweet Reprieve: One Couple's Journey to the Frontiers of Medicine* (New York: Crown Publishers, Inc., 1991), 78
[8]Barclay, *The Gospel of Luke*, 283–84.
[9]Mark 14:36.

Chapter 14

[1]Mary Grunte, coauthor of *How to Forgive When You Don't Know How*, quoted by Dianne Hales in "Three Little Words That Will Heal You," *McCall's*, June 1994, 104.
[2]Acts 7:60 (NIV).

Chapter 15

[1]Elton Trueblood, *The Lord's Prayers* (New York, Evanston,

and London: Harper and Row, 1965), 123.

[2]William Barclay, *The Daily Study Bible*, vol. 2, *The Gospel of Matthew*, 5th imp. (Edinburgh, Scotland: The Saint Andrew Press, 1965), 406–7.

[3]Trueblood, *The Lord's Prayers*, 121–22.

[4]Harold Myra, *Surprised by Children* (Grand Rapids, MI: Zondervan Publishing House, 2001), 41.

[5]Ibid.

[6]J. W. Shepard, *The Christ of the Gospels: An Exegetical Study* (Grand Rapids, MI: William. B. Eerdmans Publishing Company, 1956), 601.

[7]Psalm 69:1–3.

Chapter 16

[1]Bob Buford, *Halftime* (Grand Rapids, MI: Zondervan Publishing House, 1994), 56.

[2]E. Stanley Jones, *Victory Through Surrender* (Nashville: Abingdon Press, 1966), 110.

[3]Psalm 31:1, 5.

Chapter 17

[1]Emily Gardiner Neal, *The Healing Power of Christ* (Carmel, NY: Guideposts Associates, Inc., 1972), xii.

[2]Philip Yancey, *Where Is God When It Hurts?* (Grand Rapids, MI: Zondervan Publishing House, 1977), 119.

[3]Gerald L. Sittser, *A Grace Disguised* (Grand Rapids, MI: Zondervan Publishing House, 1996), 36–37.

[4]From the old hymn, "O Love That Wilt Not Let Me Go," words by George Matheson, 1842–1906.

Bibliography

Barclay, William. *The Daily Study Bible*. Vol. 2, *The Gospel of John*. 3rd ed. Edinburgh, Scotland: The Saint Andrew Press, 1964.

————. *The Daily Study Bible. The Gospel of Luke*. 3rd ed. Edinburgh, Scotland: The Saint Andrew Press, 1964.

————. *The Daily Study Bible. The Gospel of Mark*. 7th imp. Edinburgh, Scotland: The Saint Andrew Press, 964.

————. *The Daily Study Bible*. Vols. 1 and 2, *The Gospel of Matthew*. 6th imp. Edinburgh, Scotland: The Saint Andrew Press, 1965.

————. *The Daily Study Bible. Philippians, Colossians, and Thessalonians*. 2nd ed. Edinburgh, Scotland: The Saint Andrew Press, 1960.

————. *The Mind of Jesus*. New York: Harper and Row, 1960, 1961.

Carroll, B. H. *Messages on Prayer*. Compiled by J. W. Crowder. Edited by J. B. Cranfill. Nashville: Broadman Press, 1942.

Coleman, Robert E. *The Mind of the Master*. Old Tappan, NJ: Fleming H. Revell Company, 1977.

Corbishley, Thomas. *The Prayer of Jesus*. Garden City, NY: Doubleday and Company, Inc., 1977.

Denny, Randal Earl. *In the Shadow of the Cross*. Kansas City, MO: Beacon Hill Press of Kansas City, 1995.

Dunn, Ronald. *When Heaven Is Silent*. Nashville: Thomas Nelson Publishers, 1994.

Fosdick, Harry Emerson. *The Meaning of Prayer*. New York: Association Press, 1915.

Hazard, David. "Listening in Silence." *Charisma*, July 1996, 63.

Hester, H. I. *The Heart of the New Testament*. Nashville: Broadman Press, 1950, 1963.

Jeremias, Joachim. *The Prayers of Jesus*. Philadelphia: Fortress Press, 1967.

Jones, E. Stanley. *Victory Through Surrender*. Nashville: Abingdon Press, 1966.

Keener, Craig S. *The IVP Bible Background Commentary New Testament*. Downers Grove, IL: InterVarsity Press, 1993.

Keller, W. Phillip. "Solitude for Serenity and Strength." *Decision*, August-September 1981, 8–9.

Koessler, John M. "Keys to a Healthy Emotional Life." *Decision*, September 1991, 27–28.

Lockyer, Herbert. *All the Prayers of the Bible*. Grand Rapids, MI: Zondervan Publishing House, 1959.

Mitchell, Curtis C. *Praying Jesus' Way*. Old Tappan, NJ: Fleming H. Revell, 1977.

Morris, Leon. *Tyndale New Testament Commentaries*. Vol. 3, *The Gospel According to St. Luke*. Grand Rapids, MI: William B. Eerdmans Publishing Company, 1974.

Myra, Harold. *Surprised by Children*. Grand Rapids, MI: Zondervan, 2001.

Osborne, Millard. "The Word of Loneliness." In *The Way of the Cross and Resurrection*. Edited by John M. Drescher. Scottdale, PA: Herald Press, 1978.

Pippert, Rebecca Manley. *Hope Has Its Reasons*. New York: Harper and Row, 1989.

Poinsett, Brenda. *Not My Will but Thine*. Nashville: Broadman and Holman, 1998.

———. *When Jesus Prayed*. Nashville: Broadman Press, 1981.

———. *Prayerfully Yours*. Nashville: Broadman Press, 1979.

———. *Reaching Heaven: Discovering the Cornerstones of Jesus' Prayer Life*. Chicago: Moody Press, 2002.

Redding, David A. *Before You Call I Will Answer*. Old Tappan, NJ: Fleming H. Revell, 1985.

Robertson, A. T. *A Harmony of the Gospels for Students of the Life of Christ*. New York and London: Harper and Brothers Publishers, 1950.

Sacks, Stuart. *Hebrews Through a Hebrew's Eyes*. Baltimore: Lederer Messianic Publishers, 1995.

Shepard, J. W. *The Christ of the Gospels: An Exegetical Study*. Grand Rapids, MI: William B. Eerdmans Publishing Company, 1956.

Sittser, Gerald L. *A Grace Disguised*. Grand Rapids, MI: Zondervan Publishing House, 1996.

Summers, Ray. *Commentary on Luke*. Waco, TX: Word Books, 1972.

The Broadman Bible Commentary. Vol. 8, *Matthew–Mark*. Nashville: Broadman Press, 1969.

The Broadman Bible Commentary. Vol. 9, *Luke–John*, Nashville: Broadman Press, 1969.

Tasker, R. V. G. *Tyndale New Testament Commentaries*. Vol. 1, *The Gospel According to St. Matthew*. Grand Rapids, MI: William B. Eerdmans Publishing Company, 1961.

The Interpreter's Bible. Vol. 7. Nashville: Abingdon Press, 1955.

The Interpreter's Bible. Vol. 8. Nashville: Abingdon Press, 1955.

Thomson, James G. S. S. *The Praying Christ*. Grand Rapids, MI: William B. Eerdmans Publishing Company, 1959.

Trueblood, Elton. *The Lord's Prayers*. New York, Evanston, and London: Harper and Row, 1965.

Vigeveno, H. S. *Jesus the Revolutionary*. Glendale, CA: Regal Books, 1966.

Wuest, Kenneth S. *Wuest's Word Studies: First Peter in the Greek New Testament*. Grand Rapids, MI: William B. Eerdmans Publishing Company, 1942.

Yancey, Philip. *Where Is God When It Hurts?* Grand Rapids, MI: Zondervan Publishing House, 1977.

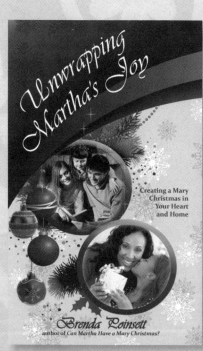

ll help you

is CHRISTMAS SEASON!

**Can Martha Have
a Mary Christmas?**
*Untangling Expectations and
Truly Experiencing Jesus*
Brenda Poinsett
ISBN-10: 1-56309-931-4
ISBN-13: 978-1-56309-931-1
$9.99 N054117

New Hope® Publishers is a division of WMU®, an international organization that challenges Christian believers to understand and be radically involved in God's mission. For more information about WMU, go to wmu.com. More information about New Hope books may be found at NewHopeDigital.com New Hope books may be purchased at your local bookstore.

Use the QR reader on your smartphone to visit us online at **NewHopeDigital.com**

If you've been blessed by this book, we would like to hear your story. The publisher and author welcome your comments and suggestions at: newhopereader@wmu.org.